Waddingtons Family Card Games

Also available in Pan Books

The Complete Patience Book Basil Dalton
Bridge for Beginners Victor Mollo and Nico Gardener
How to Play a Good Game of Bridge
Terence Reese and Albert Dormer
The Pan Book of Card Games Hubert Phillips
Play Poker to Win 'Amarillo Slim' Preston

WADDINGTONS
FAMILY CARD GAMES

ROBERT HARBIN

PAN BOOKS LONDON AND SYDNEY

First published 1972 by Elm Tree Books Ltd
This edition published 1974 by Pan Books Ltd,
Cavaye Place, London SW10 9PG
2nd printing 1975
ISBN 0 330 23892 2
© Robert Harbin 1972

Made and printed in Great Britain by
Cox & Wyman Ltd, London, Reading and Fakenham

Contents

GAMES FOR THE YOUNG

PATIENCE GAMES

SIMPLE CARD TRICKS

Foreword

A pack of cards is guaranteed to give more fun than anything else I can think of. Ever since I can remember, a pack of cards has been a source of endless enjoyment, and during my years as a professional magician an absolute necessity.

Card games of all kinds have played a big part in my life, but I have never been particularly expert at any one game. Perhaps that was because I simply could not take card-playing seriously; for me it was just fun.

When I was asked to compile a book of card games suitable for the family, I rushed around and collected numerous books on the subject: only to find that I did not possess the ability to follow the sometimes obscure and highly technical explanations. They were all Greek to me. To solve the problem, I began actually to play the games with friends and acquaintances, making notes all the time. In this way I feel that I have managed to produce something easily understandable even by the beginner. I hope, therefore, that you will be able to follow my instructions as readily as I believe you should.

On top of all this, I persuaded a friend of mine to try out every game from my first manuscript: then we compared notes and made alterations and improvements, and so it went on to the bitter end. Poor fellow, he'll never be the same again.

You will notice that throughout I refer to the players as males. This was only to facilitate the explanations. Ladies, you are more than welcome around the card-table.

During my travels in the world of card games I discovered that the most unexpected people have favourite games. I was told, for example, that Sir Winston Churchill played Bezique whenever he could. I discovered that there is a tremendous amount of card-playing going on in pubs and clubs all over Britain, and that most games are played differently in different parts of the country.

You will find, for example, that very few Cribbage 'schools' play exactly alike. It is all very confusing; so if you join in a game with strangers, check with them and adjust your play accordingly.

If after a while you decide that you would like to take up card-playing more seriously than I have provided for in this book, there is any amount of literature on the subject. You have only to look around a bookshop or library to discover this. At the end of this book you will find a few suggestions for further study, some easily obtainable, some hard to find except at antiquarian bookshops; but the list is included only in case you need it. Many experts have written many thousands of words about the more important card games, so you can expect to be helped all the way.

I hope most sincerely that you will have fun with this collection of games, and suggest, as a starter, that you try Pishti, a game which a Turkish gentleman taught me: it's fun, it's exciting. Then go on from there.

You will find enough games in this book to keep you busy for a long time. All you need now is a couple of packs of decent quality playing-cards.

ROBERT HARBIN

London

Games for two

GERMAN WHIST
Required: 1 pack of cards, pencil and paper

Two people can play this game; you need a pack of cards without Jokers, and a pencil and paper for scoring.

It isn't the greatest game in the world, but it can pass the time pleasantly on a wet day when there's nothing better to do.

You cut for deal; lowest card takes the deal, Ace counting low.

The dealer gives a card alternately to his opponent and himself until each has thirteen cards, then places the rest of the pack face down on the table and turns the top card face up. The suit of this card is trumps for that game.

The other player leads and the dealer must follow suit. If at any time you can't follow suit you can take the trick by playing a trump; a trump card, however small, beats any card of any other suit.

The two cards played are put aside face down and are of no further interest. The winner of the trick is now entitled to take the exposed card from the top of the pack and add it to his hand; the loser takes the next card without showing its face, then turns the next face up on top of the pack. The winner leads again, and so on.

Play proceeds in this way, each player building up his hand for the final battle, until all the face-down pile has gone. Then the game proper begins: winner of the last trick leads, and the object is to win as many tricks as you can with the hand you have built up. The winner is the one who has taken seven or more tricks out of the last thirteen; subtract six from the number of tricks you have won and the remainder is your score for that game. For example, if you have 9 tricks and your opponent 4, your score is 9 minus 6, i.e. 3.

Shuffle all the cards and start again, taking turns to deal.

Stop playing when you have had enough. Then each player tots up his or her score. Play for money or for fun.

Obviously this is a game of skill and there are one or two things to bear in mind. Try to remember the cards that have been played; this is important.

The exposed card on top of the pack plays a very big part in this game. If it is a card you do not need, try not to win the trick, let your opponent have it. You realize, of course, that your opponent is thinking the same way! Weigh up how good a card it is worth playing in order to secure a useful exposed card; it may for example be worth playing a high card to secure a good trump for the final game. Remember too that the unexposed card may be a good one; this is a gamble.

As with all card games in which trumps play a part, it may sometimes be a good play to 'draw' trumps if you are stronger in them than your opponent; then you can lead your 'long suit' of which your opponent has none left, and he will have to throw away his good cards at last.

Small trumps are useful in the first part of the game when you cannot follow your opponent's lead and want a good exposed card.

This is an easy game to learn and play, and it makes good practice for more difficult games.

BEZIQUE
Required: a Bezique set (or 2 packs of Piquet cards), pencil and paper

There are none too many really good card games for two players, so I very much want to recommend Bezique. It is an old game which originated in Sweden, and first came to this country just a hundred years ago; it became popular in Germany under the name Penuchle and thence spread to America where it is still widely played as Pinochle, though the rules and scoring have undergone considerable change. It is still, however, basically the same game.

In this country several variations were introduced, of which the most widely played was Rubicon Bezique, which uses four packs and has an elaborate scoring system. I find these variations a bit confusing. Fortunately, a friend of mine, who as a small boy used to play Bezique with his grandmother, has a clear recollection of the game as he learnt it, so I have got him to describe it for you.

You need two of what are known as Piquet packs; ordinary packs without the Twos, Threes, Fours, Fives, and Sixes. It is best to use special markers for scoring, though of course you can use pencil and paper. You can buy Bezique sets – my friend has a nice one which is about ninety years old; these consist of a box with the two 32-card packs, two markers like clock dials with movable hands, and a book of rules.

So here is the basic game as my friend used to play it long ago; and if you become keen on it, as I am sure you will, you can go in for Rubicon Bezique later.

Decide beforehand whether you are going to play 1,000, 1,500, or 2,000 points up. Shuffle the two packs together and cut for deal, lowest card takes the deal, Ace counting low. In subsequent deals, take turns to deal.

The non-dealer cuts the pack, and the dealer gives eight cards to each, dealing three, two and three. He then puts the rest of the pack in the middle of the table and turns up the top card at the side of it to indicate the trump suit. If this is a Seven he scores 10 points, and don't forget trumps beat anything.

The play is in two parts, the preliminary play and the play-off. In the preliminary the object is to score points by acquiring

4

and declaring certain combinations of cards; in the play-off, to take tricks which carry scoring points.

These are the declarations and the points they score:

Bezique (Queen of Spades and Jack of Diamonds): 40.
Double Bezique (Both Queens of Spades and both Jacks of Diamonds): 500.
Royal Marriage (King and Queen of trumps): 40.
Common Marriage (King and Queen of any other suit): 20.
Four Aces: 100.
Four Kings: 80.
Four Queens: 60.
Four Jacks: 40.
Sequence (Ace, King, Queen, Jack and Ten of trumps): 250.

Note that I have given the cards making up a sequence in their usual order in most card games, but it is important to remember that in Bezique the Ten is next highest to the Ace and higher than the King.

Apart from these declarations, each of the following scores 10 points:

Exchanging the Seven of trumps for the trump card.
Playing the Seven of trumps.
Winning the last trick of all.
Each Ace and Ten in the tricks you take.

This is how the preliminary play goes. The non-dealer looks at his hand and leads a card which he thinks he is least likely to need to make a declaration. The dealer can either take the trick with a higher card of the same suit, or with a trump; or can lose it by playing a lower card of the same suit, or playing a card of equal value – in which case the card led wins – or throwing away a card of a different suit. He is not compelled, in this part of the game, to follow suit.

There is no point in taking tricks at this stage of the game except when you want to make a declaration, which you can do only immediately after taking a trick; or if the trick contains an Ace or Ten.

The winner of the trick makes his declaration, if any; or if he holds the Seven of trumps he can exchange it for the turned-up trump card if he wishes, and if it is an Ace or Ten, or a card he wants to complete a Bezique or a Royal Marriage, it is well worth his while to do so. In any case he scores 10 for making the exchange.

Then the winner turns the trick face down in front of him, and each player makes his hand up to eight cards again from the pack, the winner of the trick taking the top card and the loser the next. The winner of the trick leads for the next trick.

In making declarations there are important points to remember. You place the cards in question face up in front of you and they stay there until you play them to a trick or use them for a different declaration. You can use the same card more than once in different combinations: for example, having declared the King and Queen of trumps as a Royal Marriage, you could later add the Ace, Ten, and Jack to declare a Sequence. But you cannot declare a Royal Marriage, play the King, and later declare another Royal Marriage with the same Queen and a second King. You would need a second Queen of trumps.

You could declare a Bezique, and later use the Queen to declare four Queens. But if you then played the Jack to a trick, and later laid down another Queen of Spades and Jack of Diamonds, you could not claim Double Bezique, only a second single one. For a valid declaration, all the necessary cards must be on the table at one time.

If Four Jacks have been declared, the Jack of trumps could be used again as part of a Sequence, and the Jack of Diamonds could be used for a Bezique or Double Bezique. If Four Aces have been declared, the Ace of trumps could be used to complete a Sequence. But note that once you have declared a Sequence you cannot use the King and Queen subsequently for a Royal Marriage; the Marriage must be declared first.

So the things to remember are: cards forming a declaration must be on the table together; cards once declared in a combination cannot be used again in a similar combination, only in different ones; Kings and Queens once married, or having been part of a Sequence, cannot be married again but can be used as part of a Four.

Back to the play. Let us suppose that after the deal you pick up the Ten, King, Nine and Seven of Hearts, Queen and Nine of Spades, Queen and Jack of Diamonds; and the dealer turns

6

up the Queen of Hearts for trumps. This is not a bad hand. You have a Bezique right away; and if you can exchange your Seven of trumps for the Queen, you will have three Queens towards a Four, and three cards towards a Sequence as well. It is your lead, and you want to win the first trick if you can, without spoiling your prospects. Your best lead would be the Nine of Hearts; your opponent can only take it with the Ace, Ten, King, Queen or Jack, and even if he has one of these he probably will not want to spoil his own chances by playing it at this stage.

So he throws away. (Remember that he is not compelled to follow suit.) You pick up your trick and turn the cards face down in front of you, then you exchange your Seven of Hearts for the Queen, adding the Queen to your hand and putting the Seven in its place. Score 10 for the exchange. Then you make your hand up to eight cards again by taking the top card of the pack without showing it, and your opponent does the same.

Suppose your new card is the Jack of Hearts. That's a bit of luck. You now have the Ten, King, Queen and Jack of Hearts, only needing the Ace for a Sequence; your original Bezique; and three Queens towards a Four. Next time you win a trick you can declare either your Bezique or your Royal Marriage; though at this stage there is no great hurry to make a declaration. It is your lead again; the Nine of Spades is the only card you want to play, so down it goes.

Your opponent takes it with the Ten of Spades. This will count 10 points to him later, when you both reckon up the Aces and Tens in your tricks. He then declares a Common Marriage, the King and Queen of Diamonds. Your pick-up card is the Eight of Hearts; no use to you for a declaration, but you can very likely take the next trick with it and then declare your Bezique.

So the play goes. You score your points as you go, apart from the Aces and Tens in your tricks; it is most convenient to leave these until the end of the hand. You will find that you are constantly being faced with the difficult decision of what card to lead or play to a trick; you may not want to part with any of your cards. You have to weigh up your chances. For example, after you have declared your Bezique you may decide that the chance of picking up another Queen of Spades and Jack of Diamonds to make a Double Bezique are slim, compared with

7

the chance of completing your Sequence or your Four Queens. So you would play the Jack of Diamonds in preference to any of your other cards.

All the time, you are weighing up the cards your opponent has already declared and deducing what he holds. Suppose, for example, he plays a King of trumps. That probably means that he holds both Kings of trumps, or he would not part with it; so you can give up any hope of completing a Sequence or a Royal Marriage, and concentrate on another declaration.

As you get towards the last of the preliminary eight tricks, and the end of the pack, it may pay you to win a trick at the cost of spoiling a promising declaration in order to get another declaration made. Also, you want to prevent your opponent from making his declarations. So you might abandon the hope of getting an Ace of trumps to complete a Sequence, play the Ten of trumps to win a trick, and be content with declaring a Royal Marriage. Or if you have a completed Sequence but intended to declare the Royal Marriage first, you may have to abandon the Marriage and get the Sequence in before it is too late.

Well: you have come to the end of the pack, made and scored your declarations, and all that remains is the play-off. Now the winner of the last trick leads. Remember that a player is now obliged to follow suit or trump, and he is also obliged to win the trick if he can; though of course if he can neither follow suit nor trump he will have to throw away.

You have two objects: to win tricks containing Aces and Tens, each of which scores 10 points to you, and to take the last trick which also scores 10. When it is all over, you and your opponent gather up your tricks and go through them counting up the Aces and Tens and add the points to your score. Once it comes to the play-off you have finished with declarations, of course; it is most exasperating to be left with a scoring combination which you have been unable to declare, but you just have to grin and bear it.

So you and your opponent tot up your total scores, and if neither of you has reached 1,000, or whatever you agreed on for game, you shuffle the pack thoroughly and play a fresh deal.

I have tried to explain Bezique clearly; I hope that I have not made it seem complicated. It isn't, actually; if you just try one game you will find it quite simple, and quite fascinating. I don't mind betting that it will become your favourite game.

PIQUET

Required: 1 pack of Piquet Cards, pencil and paper or (cribbage board).

Piquet is a two-player game for the connoisseur of card play, calling for great care and judgement, yet with much depending on the luck of the deal.

But it is an elegant, courtly kind of game, which has existed almost unaltered for long enough to be regarded as a classic; its inclusion in this book is justified on that account alone. Almost certainly of French origin, Piquet has been played in Britain since the early sixteenth century, and in France before that. Its terminology is mainly French; so of course is its name, which is why it grates on me to hear people referring to it as 'Pe-kett' or worse still, 'Picket'. Please yourself: but it's 'Pe-kay' to me.

Piquet, as you will see, has much in common with Bezique, which probably derives from it, and which I personally prefer as a game for two players. Like Bezique, it can be enjoyed for its own sake without playing for money.

A pack of 32 cards is used. You can buy Piquet sets of two packs, or alternatively take out the Sixes, Fives, Fours, Threes and Twos from your regular pack.

The cards rank as in Bridge: Ace highest, then King, Queen, Jack, Ten, Nine, Eight, and Seven lowest. There are no trumps and all suits are of equal value.

Scoring can be done with pencil and paper, or a cribbage board, but in practice experienced players usually announce scores and running totals aloud as the points are made, simply noting down the result at the end of each deal.

Now let's look at the terms used, and at the same time get an idea of the play and scoring.

A *partie* is a complete game of six deals, three by each player alternately. The dealer is known as the *minor* or *younger* hand; the non-dealer as the *major* or *elder* hand. On each deal the dealer is at some disadvantage; so as the players have to take turns to deal it is a good thing to deal first, because then you have your advantage on the sixth and often crucial deal.

So you cut for deal, lowest card deals. Twelve cards are dealt to each player, singly, or in twos, or however you decide. The remaining eight cards are placed on the table in two face-down fans, of five and three cards.

These eight cards are known as the *talon,* the group of five being the *major* portion and that of three the *minor*.

Now, the scoring for each deal comes under two headings: the points made by *declarations* from the hand, based on certain combinations of cards, and those made during subsequent play of the hand.

If after the deal either player has a hand containing no Kings, Queens, or Jacks, he may if he wishes claim 10 points for *carte blanche*. It is not always an advantage to disclose the fact; but if you don't claim carte blanche right away you can't score the 10 points. In some circumstances it is worth your while to forgo them.

Each player examines his hand and decides what to discard. Major hand (the non-dealer) must discard at least one card, and any number up to five. He has to consider how to build up his hand to best advantage in respect both of the declarations and the subsequent play. Discards are placed face downwards before him; the other player does not see them but the discarder may refer to them at any time if he forgets what they are. Then he picks up an equivalent number from the major part of the talon.

The same rule applies to minor hand, except that if major hand has exchanged his full five cards, minor is limited to the other three, the minor portion. If however major hand has exchanged less than five, minor can exchange any or all of those remaining; but he takes them in order as they lie, i.e. the balance of the major portion first. Any cards remaining in the talon after the exchanging has been completed may be inspected by minor hand, but only after the first lead has been made; he does so by turning them face up so that major hand can see them also.

Making the right discards is a vital part of the game and calls for difficult decisions. An intelligent player can get a very accurate idea, as the declarations proceed, of the constitution of his opponent's hand.

Now for the declarations. These are always made in the same order and with certain formalities. First, *point*. This is the greatest number of cards in any one suit. Say major hand's longest suit is Spades, of which he holds five: he will announce 'Point of five'.

If minor hand has no suit longer than four cards he says

'Good', and major hand scores 5 points, one for each card. If minor hand too has a five-card suit he asks 'How many?' Major hand replies with the *point value* of his long suit, reckoning 11 for an Ace, 10 each for court cards, and the face value of the other cards: A K J 8 7 would give a point value of 46.

If minor hand's point value is less he says 'Good' and major still scores his 5 points. If it is equal, neither scores. But if it is greater, or if minor hand has, say, a six-card suit, he says, 'Not good' and scores accordingly.

There is only one point score, and that only for one player; if you had, say, two five-card suits, you would score only for the one you have elected to declare.

You are not, by the way, compelled to declare every scoring combination: there are occasions, as you will see, when it is inadvisable to do so.

The point settled, major hand next declares his best *sequence*. The sequences, and scores, are:

Tierce: a sequence of three cards, e.g. Queen, Jack, Ten, scoring three.

Quart: a sequence of four cards, scoring four.

Quint: a sequence of five cards, scoring fifteen.

Sixième or Sextet: a sequence of six cards, scoring sixteen.

Septième or Septet: a sequence of seven cards, scoring seventeen.

Huitième or Octet: a sequence of eight cards, scoring eighteen.

The same procedure as for point is again followed. Major may hold, say, Ace, King and Queen of Hearts. He will announce 'Tierce'. If minor hand hasn't a tierce he will say 'Good'. If he has, say, Queen, Jack and Ten of Spades he will ask 'How good?' Major will in this case reply, 'Top tierce', meaning Ace high, and gain the 3 points. If minor has, say, Ace, King and Queen of Diamonds he will say 'Equal' and neither will score. But if he holds a quart or better he will say 'Not good' and score it.

The player who scores the highest sequence may then announce, and score, any lesser sequences. For example, if minor hand has established his quart, as above, and also holds a tierce in another suit, he scores 4+3=7 points.

11

So it could happen that a player who holds Ace, King and Queen in each of the four suits might score nothing for sequences, if his opponent holds Ten, Nine, Eight and Seven of one suit.

Now major hand declares any *groups* or *sets* he holds: that is, three or four cards of like value. Three Aces, three Kings, three Queens or three Jacks score 3; the Tens and lower groups do not count. But four Kings, Queens, Jacks and in this case four Tens, score 14.

The same procedure is again followed. Major declares, say, 'Three Kings'. Minor will say 'Good' if he has nothing better, or 'Not good' if he holds, for example, four Queens. And as before, a player who has established his top group may then score for any other groups he holds as well.

At this point, one or both players have amassed a certain number of points, which they announce. Major hand may, shall we say, have 5 for point and 17 (14+3) for groups; total 22. Minor may have 5 for a quint sequence, total 5.

The player who does not score point may ask his opponent to state in which suit his point is; similarly with sequences.

It is possible that a player may amass 30 points before his opponent has scored at all, either at this point in the game, or later during play. If it happens after the lead has been made to the first trick, he can claim *pique*, adding another 30 points to his score; but if he has made up his 30 points during the declarations part of the hand, before play begins, it is called *repique* and scores an additional 60 points instead of 30.

Major hand's declaration completed, the play of the deal begins. Major hand leads first: then minor hand makes any declaration he may have; then minor hand plays to the lead. Thereafter the winner of each trick leads to the next. Players must follow suit if possible, though if they have a choice they may either win or lose the trick as they wish; if they cannot follow suit they throw away.

Players score 1 point for leading to a trick, and 1 point for taking a trick from the opponent's lead. The winner of the last trick scores an extra point, and the winner of the most tricks scores 10 points for *cards*.

If each player has taken six tricks there is no score for cards. If one player takes all the twelve tricks he scores 40 points for *capot,* instead of, not in addition to, the 10 for cards.

12

There is just one other term to explain, and a very important one: *rubicon*. This used to be known in Britain as lurch: hence the expression 'left in the lurch', as in the old music-hall song.

If at the end of the partie one player has failed to score 100 points, his total score, plus 100 points, is added to that of his opponent. This occurrence is called a rubicon (the river Julius Caesar crossed, remember?) and the losing player is said to be rubiconed.

Obviously, this disaster is to be avoided if possible. You will see now why it is advantageous to deal first and so make sure of being the major hand on the last vital deal.

If after the fifth deal a player finds that he is far short of the necessary 100 points, he must do all he can to make his score up to 100; he may feel inclined to speculate boldly in the matter of his discards, for example. As you will see presently, it may be better to lose heavily than by only a small margin if you must lose.

If the rubicon appears inevitable, then the obvious thing to do is to score the minimum possible on the last deal to avoid presenting the opponent with more points than need be. The player in this position will try to contrive that during the play of the last deal he and his opponent make six tricks each, so that there is no score for cards; he will even forgo a capot if the 40 points he gets for it still do not make his score up to 100, though this situation is unlikely. More usually, he will forgo winning declarations: if the opponent has declared a tierce, for example, and he holds a quart, he will ignore it and say 'Equal' so that neither scores anything for sequences. Or he will ignore a carte blanche. This may seem a bit unethical, but it is quite permissible.

Apart from the rubicon situation: if neither player reaches 100 points at the end of the partie, the one with the higher score adds his opponent's score to his own, plus another 100 points.

If each player scores over 100 points, the player with the higher score subtracts his opponent's score from his own and adds another 100 points.

So, at the end of the partie, three examples of the final scoring:

(a) A scores 150, B scores 130. A wins by 20 + 100 = 120 points.

13

(b) A scores 350, B scores 90. A wins 350 + 90 + 100 = 540 points.

(c) A scores 96, B scores 93. A wins 96 + 93 + 100 = 289 points.

Example (b) is the rubicon.

One other thing about the scoring that I should mention. If a player has declared carte blanche his opponent cannot, of course, claim a pique or repique; nor if there has been equality in respect of a point or sequence.

Now let's look at a sample deal. I am assuming that it is my deal; I shuffle the pack and deal as follows.

You have: Spades: Ace, Eight, Seven. Hearts: Ace, King, Jack. Diamonds: Queen, Jack, Seven. Clubs: King, Jack, Ten.

I have: Spades: King, Jack Ten. Hearts: Queen, Ten, Nine. Diamonds: Ace, King, Ten. Clubs: Ace, Nine, Seven.

I have not 'set up' contrived hands to illustrate particular points, and I may make errors of judgement in the discards and play: we'll just assume that you and I are beginners learning the game.

You, as major hand, examine your cards. At the moment you have three of each suit, no sequences, nothing better in the way of groups than three Jacks.

You decide to discard the Eight and Seven of Spades and all three Diamonds, in the hope of improving your hand. It means losing one of your Jacks but it seems the best compromise. You lay these five cards face down in front of you and pick up the major talon.

Now your hand is, Spades: Ace, Queen, Nine; Hearts: Ace, King, Jack, Seven; Diamonds: Eight; Clubs: King, Queen, Jack, Ten. A bit disappointing: it could have been worse!

I discard the Nine and Seven of Clubs and the Ten of Diamonds. I pick up the Eight of Hearts, Eight of Clubs, Nine of Diamonds. Well, I've definitely ended up with a mediocre lot.

You declare a point of four. I ask 'How good?' You count up the point value of your Clubs – higher than your Hearts – and say '40'. The best I can do with my Hearts is 37, so I say 'Good' and you score 4 for point.

Now you claim a quart for your Clubs. I say 'Good' again and you score another 4, total 8.

14

Neither of us can claim anything for groups; so no score here. Maybe you are wishing you had that Queen and Jack of Diamonds that you discarded! As for me, I have nothing to declare.

You lead AH, saying '9' (8 for your declarations, 1 for the lead). I play 8H. You lead KH saying '10'; I play 9H. You switch to KC saying '11'; I take it with the Ace saying '1', my first score. I lead AD saying '2'; you play 8D. I follow with KD; that's '3'; you play 9S – difficult to know what to throw away. I lead 9D saying '4'; you play 7H. I lead QH saying '5'; you play JH. I lead 10H saying '6'; you play QS. I lead KS saying '7'; you take it with your Ace, saying '12', and lead your Clubs, making 15 plus 1 for the last trick, total 16. Six tricks each, so nothing for cards.

So now we book down our totals, 16 for you, 6 for me; nothing much in it at the end of the first deal.

Well, that gives you an idea of how it goes. I am tempted to play through an entire illustrative partie, in the hope that all the various contingencies would arise: I could of course contrive the hands to make sure they did.

But it would take pages and pages, including all the comments and explanations, and on consideration I really don't think it's justified. If you want, after reading all the foregoing, to tackle Piquet – and I hope that all the rules haven't put you off – it would be far better to find a beginner like yourself and play a partie or two, referring to the previous pages whenever either of you is in doubt.

That would be the quickest, and soundest, way to learn. So go ahead, and the best of luck.

Or should I say 'bonne chance'?

KALABRIASZ ('CLOBIOSH')
Required: 1 pack of cards, pencil and paper

In a little restaurant in Ivor Place, London, NW1, you can always meet lots of taxi-drivers and good fellows from all walks of life, taking refreshment. Ray Inzani, son of the proprietor, is an engaging host: known for his earthy wit, his baffling card tricks, and his love for a game of Clobiosh at the end of the day.

This game, possibly of Hungarian origin, has retained much of its native terminology, but differs here and there from the game played on the Continent. In fact, there are as many variations in the rules and the manner of play as there are in the name itself. Some variations are for three or four players, but I am settling for the two-handed game as I learnt it, an ideal game for two.

You play with a Piquet pack: that is, a pack from which the Sixes, Fives, Fours, Threes, and Twos have been removed.

Clobiosh, which is what we will call it, is not unlike Bezique (*see* p 4). At first sight it seems to be a fairly simple game, but after a while you will realize that it calls for considerable skill. Before you start have a glance at the previous section on Bezique, and you will have something to work on.

As in Bezique, you score for combinations or 'melds' rather than for the number of tricks won.

The ranking of the cards is important to the game and must be thoroughly understood to begin with. In the trump suit, the highest card is the Jack, called *Jass*; then the Nine, called *Menel*; then the Ace, Ten, King, Queen, Eight, and Seven, in that order, the Seven being the lowest. In other suits, the Ace is highest, then Ten, King, Queen, Jack, Nine, Eight, and Seven.

The King and Queen of trumps, together, are known as 'Bella' or 'Ballot' – this possibly comes from the French game of Belotte.

Let us assume that you and I are playing. We cut for deal; lowest card deals. I cut the lower card, so as dealer I shuffle the pack, pass it to you to cut, you cut it towards me, I complete the cut and deal: three cards to you, three to me, three more to you, three more to me. I put the rest of the pack, the 'talon', on the table, turn up the next (the top) card and place it beside the

16

talon. In subsequent deals, the winner of the last game is dealer for the next.

Now we look at our six cards and first of all consider whether it will suit us to have the suit of the turned-up card as trumps. You as non-dealer have the first option. If you are satisfied with that suit, you say 'I accept'. If not, you say 'Pass'. Now I have the chance of accepting or passing. If either of us accepts, then the suit of the turned-up card will be trumps for that game.

If I pass, then you have the option of nominating another suit as trumps. If you pass again, the option passes to me. If I pass, we throw in our hands and you, the non-dealer that time, deal afresh.

But if one of us has established a trump suit, then I deal another three cards to each of us, then turn up the bottom card of the talon. This card plays no part in the game, it simply signifies that the deal is concluded.

If the suit of the turned-up card has been accepted as trumps, and either of us holds the Seven of that suit, he has the option of exchanging it for the turned-up card.

Now, before we go on to the play of the cards, let us have a look at the scoring combinations. Sequences are declared and scored before the play proper starts. Note that for the purposes of sequences the cards take their customary order, viz. Ace, King, Queen, Jack, Ten, Nine, Eight, Seven, and not the ranking order I've given earlier. A sequence of four scores 50; a sequence of three cards, 20. Sequences are assessed according to their highest cards, so a sequence of Ace, King, Queen of the same suit ranks higher than King, Queen, Jack of another suit. Queen, Jack, Ten, Nine of trumps ranks higher than Queen, Jack, Ten, Nine of a non-trump suit.

Bella, or Ballot, is scored during play, being declared when the second of the two cards – the King and Queen of trumps – is played; it scores 20.

Other scoring cards are scored by the player who takes the tricks containing them. These are:

Jass, the Jack of trumps:	20
Menel, the Nine of trumps:	14
Any Ace:	11
Any Ten:	10
Any King:	4

Any Queen:	3
Any Jack other than Jass:	2

Apart from this, the winning of tricks counts nothing, except that the winner of the last trick scores 10.

The game is usually played 500 up, i.e. the first player to reach 500 points is the winner.

Well: back to the play. First you, the non-dealer, declare the points value of any sequence you hold – or if you have more than one, the best sequence. Only one of us can score for sequences, and that is the one who holds the highest sequence; he scores not only for that sequence but for any others he holds, while the opponent scores nothing.

Suppose you hold a sequence of four, e.g. King, Queen, Jack, Ten of trumps, and another Queen-high sequence of four. You would say '50'. Now, if I did not hold anything better than a sequence of three, I would say 'Good' and you would score 50 for each sequence.

If I also had a sequence of four, however, say King, Queen, Jack, Ten of a non-trump suit, I would ask 'How high?' You would reply 'King high'. Your sequence would rank highest for two reasons: first because it is in trumps, but in any case, because if both held equal sequences, the non-dealer as first to declare takes precedence. But if I held an Ace-high sequence of four, I would say 'Ace high' and then I would score the 50 – plus the value of any other sequence I held.

So it is possible, and in fact often happens, for a player who holds a single sequence of four, say Jack, Ten, Nine, Eight of one suit, to score 50 for it while his opponent with three Ace-high sequences of three scores nothing.

If however you have no sequences to declare, then I declare and score whatever I have.

A player is not obliged to declare all his sequences, or indeed any, if he thinks that his opponent's hand is likely to be better and it will pay him to keep quiet and conceal the value of his hand for the play.

Sequences declared and scored, the play begins, you as non-dealer leading. A trick of course consists of two cards, one played by each of us. The second player to trick must follow suit if he can. If he cannot, he must play a trump if he has one. If he can neither follow suit nor trump, he can throw away any

18

card. If a trump is led the second player must win the trick with a higher one if he can. If not he must follow suit unless he has no trumps.

Each trick is of course won by the highest card, remembering the ranking value which I gave you at the beginning. And a trump beats any non-trump card. The winner of each trick places it face down in front of him and leads to the next. And remember, the idea is to take tricks containing the scoring cards.

When all the nine tricks have been played, the deal is over. Now both players tot up their scores: 50's and 20's for the sequences declared at the beginning, 20 for Ballot if declared, 10 for the winner of the last trick, and the various scores for the scoring cards they have taken. Now comes a rather peculiar reckoning.

If the 'bidder', that is the player who decided the trump suit, has a higher score than his opponent, each scores his own total. If however the non-bidder has the higher score, he scores the whole of his points plus those of his opponent, who gets nothing. This is called 'going bate'.

And if the two players have equal scores, then the non-bidder scores his own points and the bidder scores nothing. This is 'going half-bate'.

So you will see, if you think about it, why there is that option of passing at the start. You have to be jolly sure of a good hand when you nominate the trump suit, because of this danger of losing everything. For this reason experienced players pass and 'throw in' as many hands as they play out, or even more.

I have described a pretty simple version of the game, as I learnt it. There is an even simpler version played in America which they call Clob or Klob or Clab or any one of several similar names. But if you feel that Kalabriasz is the game for you – and be assured that it is a game calling for a very high degree of skill – I recommend you to acquire *Card Games for Two* (see the bibliography at the end of this book) by Kenneth Konstam, who has written a wonderful article on the pure game and the strategy employed.

GIN RUMMY
Required: 1 pack of cards, pencil and paper

This variation of rummy is included because it is widely played, especially in America, and is an ideal game for two players. As this is essentially a gambling game it is as well to have a little money around to create an interest.

Who deals first is decided by cutting the pack; the player who cuts the lowest card deals. Ace is low, and if cards of equal value are cut, Spades rank highest, Hearts next, Diamonds next, and Clubs lowest. Apart from this the suits are no different in value in the game. After the first deal the winner of each round takes the next deal.

The dealer shuffles the pack, the opponent cuts it, and the dealer completes the cut. He then deals ten cards singly to his opponent and himself, places the rest of the pack face down on the table, and turns the top card face up beside the pack.

Each player in turn, beginning with the non-dealer, takes either the face-up card, or the unknown top card of the pack, into his hand, and then discards one card face up beside the pack. Some players allow the discard pile to be spread out so that all the cards in it can be seen; but it makes for a better game if it is kept squared up so that only the face card is visible.

There is a special point about the first turn of all, however. The non-dealer may take the face-up card if he wishes, but if he doesn't want it he cannot take the top card on the pack instead; he must say 'Pass' and the dealer has the opportunity of taking the face-up card. If he does so, the dealer in effect gets first turn; if he too rejects it, then the non-dealer can take the top card of the pack.

So the play proceeds, each player in turn taking one card and discarding one, until one player goes down and points for the deal are scored. Then a fresh deal is made, and so on to the end of that game.

The object, as in other Rummy games, is to meld your hand of ten cards into groups or 'sets' containing not less than three cards. These can be three or four cards of the same value, e.g. three Fours, three Queens, four Eights, and so on: or sequences of the same suit, e.g. King, Queen, Jack of Hearts, or Four, Three, Two, Ace of Diamonds. Note that an Ace always counts as a One, so Ace, King, Queen is not a valid sequence, but Three, Two, Ace is.

Any unmatched cards, i.e. those not forming part of a set, count against you: Kings, Queens, Jacks, and Tens each count 10 points, Aces one point, and other cards their face value.

You can go down or meld out whenever you have 10 points or less against you in unmatched cards, not before; though you are not compelled to do so immediately. The limit is sometimes set at 15 points, but 10 is recommended; this you must decide at the start.

Suppose that you decide to 'knock' or go down with 6 points against you in unmatched cards. You say 'Down for Six' and lay down your hand face up, separating the sets and unmatched cards so that your opponent can clearly see what you hold. Your opponent similarly lays down his hand face up.

If you go down with no unmatched cards at all, this is 'going gin' and you call 'Gin'. In this case you get a bonus of 25 points plus your opponent's total in unmatched cards.

If, however, you have some unmatched cards, then, before the scores are reckoned, the opponent has the privilege of reducing his 'dead wood' – the unmatched cards which count against him – by 'laying off' any he can on your sets. For example, if he has an unmatched Ten of Hearts he can lay it off on your set of the other three Tens, or on your sequence of King, Queen, Jack of Hearts, or Nine, Eight, Seven of Hearts. But he may not lay off on a gin hand.

Back to the case where you have 'gone down for six'. You may have put down two sets of cards of like value, and a sequence of three, and have just a Six unmatched. Your opponent, after doing any laying off he can, is left with a Nine, two Fives, and a Two unmatched. His total is therefore 21; from this deduct your 6, leaving you a net score on the hand of 15.

If you had 'gone gin', your score would have been your opponent's 21, plus any other unmatched cards which in this case he would have been unable to lay off, plus your bonus of 25.

Suppose, however, you go down as soon as your total in unmatched cards reaches 10; and after your opponent has laid off any unmatched cards his total is also 10, or even less. Then he has 'undercut' you, and he gets a bonus of 25 points, plus the difference between his count and yours, if any. That's a chance you have to take.

If you 'go gin' you cannot, of course, be undercut. You may think it a good idea to postpone going out as long as you can, in order to reduce your count as low as possible with the idea of undercutting your opponent. That's all very well, but remember that if he goes gin you are hoist with your own petard.

One more thing before we explain the rest of the scoring. As soon as a player goes down, and the scores have been entered, that deal is completed and the winner gathers up all the cards, shuffles, and deals afresh. But let us suppose that you are getting to the end of the pack and neither player has gone down. The last two cards of the pack are never drawn; if the player who draws the fiftieth card has discarded and still neither player can go down, then the deal is abandoned without scoring and the same player shuffles and deals again.

The game is 100 up; that is to say, as soon as a player reaches 100 points or more he wins a game. He then gets a game bonus of 100 points, or if his opponent has not scored at all (known as 'being whitewashed') the game bonus is 200 points. And for each deal won during the game, each player scores 20 points. It is usual to enter the scores cumulatively, which makes it easy to see when the game is over; and in entering the total, to deduct the number of deals won by the loser from those won by the winner and enter the difference times 20 points. Here is a sample score-sheet:

Player A	Player B		
15		First deal	
	26	Second deal	
36		Third deal	(15 + 21)
59		Fourth deal	(36 + 23)
	41	Fifth deal	(26 + 15)
66		Sixth deal	(59 + 7)
	76	Seventh deal	(41 + 35)
102		Eighth deal	(66 + 36)
100		Add for Game Bonus	
40		Five deals won, less three by opponent, 2 @ 20	
242		Total points for A	
76		Less B's total	
166		A's net score for the game.	

22

Pages could be written about the strategy of Gin Rummy. But you can learn more by playing a few games, and using your brain and your common sense, than by reading about it. Some things will be obvious with a little thought. For example: you hold the Eight of Hearts, Eight of Spades, Seven of Spades. There are four cards which will enable you to make a meld: the Eight of Clubs and Eight of Diamonds, either of which will give you three Eights; and the Nine of Spades and Six of Spades, either of which will give you a sequence. So as long as none of those four cards are in your opponent's hand, or are buried in the discard pile, your little lot is worth holding on to.

On the other hand, if you hold the King and Jack of Clubs, there is only one card, the Queen of Clubs, which will complete the sequence.

So you weigh up your chances, trying to remember what cards have gone, and watching your opponent's discards to try to assess his hand. You try to judge whether it is best to take the face card, or take a chance on the unknown top card of the pack. As your hand improves you will often find it advisable to reduce your count by taking a low card and discarding a high one. You try to judge whether to go down as soon as possible and catch your opponent with a high count, or hang on a bit in the hope of going gin, or undercutting him, or at least reducing your count. On the whole, it's a good idea to go down with only two sets and three or four low unmatched cards, rather than try for a third set and perhaps get caught. But all these points you must judge for yourself.

Gin Rummy is much like other forms of Rummy (*see* pp 69–81), but because of the subtle differences it becomes a very exciting game for two, and this is what makes it so popular. You agree to play for (shall we say?) a penny a point – but that's big gambling; perhaps a penny for every 10 points would be wiser – and then all you have to do is to pay up and make the best of it.

FIVE-CARD CRIBBAGE

Required: 1 pack of cards, cribbage-board
(or pencil and paper)

The game of 'Crib' is played throughout the length and breadth of Britain. Five-card Cribbage is a game for two players, and is the most popular version.

You require a pack of 52 cards, and for convenience you should have a Cribbage-board for scoring. You could at a pinch use pencil and paper, but it just would not be the same. Some Cribbage-boards also form a box to keep the cards in. The boards have small holes, arranged in sections of ten, into which small pegs fit, usually red for one player and white for the other; each player has two pegs, which overtake one another, so to speak, as the score mounts. So each player can see at a glance how the game is progressing.

Many years ago I came to England from South Africa on a little passenger-cum-cargo boat called the *Umvoti*. It had at one time been sunk by enemy action, but was refloated and sailed for many more years. Well: it was a five-week journey, and I learnt to play Cribbage with the crew.

To enjoy Cribbage, indeed to play at all, you must have the scoring off pat. Cribbage is all scoring; the whole fun is scoring, and the game itself revolves around the score.

Country folk are great Cribbage players, and I can assure you that no matter how good your cards are, a wily player will make circles round you. I know a little Lancashire man who, you would swear, was plain stupid. You would have great difficulty in holding an intelligent conversation with him: if you asked him what was the square root of 16, or the capital of Portugal, I'm sure he couldn't tell you. But I've watched him playing Cribbage, and he's a genius: he has only to glance at his cards in the show or crib and he'll peg up while I'm still laboriously working it all out.

All this to get you interested. Now let's talk about the details of the game. A game is 61 up, which completes the board. So with the pegs in the starting positions, cut for deal; lowest card takes the deal, Ace low. If both players cut cards of equal value, they cut again.

The dealer shuffles the pack and places it in front of his opponent, who cuts it towards the dealer, who completes the cut and deals five cards each, one at a time. Right away the scoring begins: the non-dealer pegs himself 'three for last', this being to compensate for a theoretical advantage in being the dealer.

The hands are picked up and studied. To understand your hand you must understand the scoring: but we'll come to this in a moment; first let's go through the motions. Each player discards two cards, face down, in a little heap called the 'crib' or 'box' which always belongs to the dealer. So the non-dealer carefully discards cards which he thinks will give the least possible help to the dealer, and the dealer discards two which will be useful at a later stage of the game.

The balance of the pack is now cut once more by the non-dealer and the top card of the lower half is turned face up. This card, called the 'start', plays a very important part in the game. If it happens to be a Jack, the dealer at once pegs 'two for his heels'.

Each player now has three cards, and play begins. The non-dealer leads a card, then the dealer plays one, and so on, each player in turn trying to score. All six cards are played, unless a card will bring the total value of the cards played to more than 31, as you will see.

All court cards count as 10, Ace counts 1, and other cards have their face value.

Now for the scoring in play. A player who plays a card which matches that just played by his opponent scores 'two for a pair'. Say the non-dealer leads off with a Two; if the dealer plays a Two he pegs up 'two for a pair'. Then if the first player follows with a third Two he scores 'six for pairs royal'; you see, three cards make three different pairs, viz. A and B, B and C, A and C.

If on top of that the dealer should play the fourth Two, he pegs up 'twelve for double pairs royal', for four cards make six different pairs.

But in practice you don't hear the terms 'pairs', 'pairs royal', and so on being used. The first player as he puts down his card will say 'Six', the second will say 'Twelve for two', the first 'Eighteen for six', the second 'Twenty-four for twelve'.

So much for pairs. Now for runs. These may seem a bit complicated. A run is a sequence of cards of consecutive value. Three of them score 'three for a run', which can then be extended to four for four, five for five, and even six for six. Note

25

that the cards do not need to be in order. The first player may play a Six, the second a Seven, then the first a Five, pegging three for the run. Now the second player may play an Eight, pegging four, and so on. But it is not necessary for a run of four to be preceded by a run of three; a run may not, perhaps, be completed until the last card is played: say, for example, the cards fall Three, Seven, Five, Four, and the last player plays a Six pegging 'five for the run'.

So remember, runs can be scored in any order: you have to watch out for them. And by the way, although all court cards have the same value, 10, they hold their rank where runs are concerned: King, Queen, Jack, Ten.

Now for fifteens. If a player plays a card which brings the value of the last card played up to a total of 15, he scores 'fifteen two'. Say, for example, he plays a Six on to a Nine, or a Five on to a Queen. The same applies if he plays the last of any number of cards totalling 15: for example, a Seven after four Twos. Of course, as well as pegging 'fifteen two' he might with the same card also pick up 'two for a pair', or 'three for a run'; if, for example, the play went Three, Six, Six, or Four, Five, Six.

Finally: the total value of all the cards played must not exceed 31. If for example the total stands at 29 and you can play a Two, you peg 2 points for making exactly 31. But if you had nothing less than a Three, you can't play and have to say 'Go'. If your opponent can now play a Two, he pegs the 2 points; but if he can play at all, which in this case would have to be an Ace, he scores 'one for last'. And as you can't play, play stops.

Let's just look at two examples of play. Say I, the dealer, hold Queen, Eight and Six, and you hold Seven, Five and Four. You lead the Four. I play the Six. You play your Five, pegging 'three for a run' and 'fifteen two'. I play my Eight. You play the Seven, scoring 'five for a run'. Now the total value of the cards played is 30; we both have to say 'No' and you score 'one for last'. You've done pretty well on that deal!

Another example: I as dealer hold Nine, Six, Two; you hold Nine, Four, Ace. You play your Four; I play the Two. You play your Nine and peg 'fifteen two'. I play my Nine, scoring 'two for a pair'. You play your Ace; I play my Six scoring 'two for 31'.

The play concluded, we come to the 'show'. By the way, when playing our cards we have kept them in front of us, not putting them on top of the opponent's cards. The scoring in this part of the game is similar to that in the play, except that the start card becomes a part of each player's show in turn, and also part of the dealer's crib.

The non-dealer's hand is considered first. The score is built up in every possible way. Points are always scored in a set sequence: fifteens, pairs, runs, a flush, and 'his nob'.

We already understand the first three. A flush is when all three cards in a player's hand are of the same suit, and this scores 3 points; but if the start card is also of that suit, the score is 4 points. 'His nob', which scores 1 point, is scored by a player who holds the Jack of the same suit as the start card.

Let us see what your show would score in the first example above, supposing that the start was a Three. You held, remember, Seven, Five, and Four. You must spot every possible combination and peg up your score: don't worry about overscoring; your opponent will be watching to see that you don't.

For the Seven, Five, and Three you score 'fifteen two'. And for the Three, Four, and Five you score 'three for a run'. That's all; you don't have a flush because your cards are not all of the same suit.

But suppose the 'start' was a Five, and you held two Fours and a Six. You can count the same card over and over again in different combinations. So you peg 'fifteen four' (that's the Six and Five with each of the Fours), plus 'two for a pair' (of Fours), plus twice 'three for a run' (again, the Six and Five with each of the Fours). That's 12 points altogether: pretty good!

Now to take an extreme example: suppose with your hand and the start card together, you had a Ten and three fives. (Unlikely – but just suppose.) You would score 'fifteen eight' plus a pair royal, total 14 points. Can you see how that is made up?

After the non-dealer has pegged up his show score, the dealer does the same, in exactly the same way. But he hasn't finished; he still has his crib to score, again in combination with the start card. This is where the dealer's advantage comes in. His crib may be worth nothing, but on the other hand it could be worth anything up to a theoretical maximum of 29 points – that could happen if the start was a Five, and the crib comprised the other

27

three Fives along with the Jack of the same suit as the start.

There would be eight fifteens, four made up of the Jack and different Fives, and four of three Fives. And a double pair royal; and 'one for his nob'. $16+12+1=29$.

For this to happen the dealer would have to have uncanny luck, and his opponent would have to have contributed two Fives to his crib. You may think the opponent would be crazy to do such a thing; but suppose that his original five cards were two Sevens, two Fives and an Ace? He might well discard the Fives to leave himself with a pair and one fifteen.

The possible scoring combinations in the crib seem endless, but let us just look at a few to give you the idea.

Any combination of Nines and Sixes scores 20. For example, two Nines and three Sixes. That's six different fifteens, or fifteen twelve; plus one pair and one pair royal; $12+2+6$.

Two Eights, a Four, and two Threes: $8+4+3=15$, so you have 8 for fifteens, plus two pairs, total 12.

A Six, two Fives, and two Fours, $6+5+4=15$, and that is also a run. So you peg up 8 for fifteens, 4 for pairs, and 12 for the four possible runs, total 24. Get the idea?

You have to look out for every conceivable combination.

By the way, for a flush to be scored in the crib, all five cards have to be of the same suit; it's possible, but it doesn't often happen.

To play good Cribbage you must give the game a good deal of thought. The best players seem to play instinctively, and so will you if you play regularly. Here are some pointers.

As dealer, give some thought to the cards you throw into your crib. You want cards there which will help your score at the show, and keep those which will help with the play.

As non-dealer, try to discard cards likely to be useless to the dealer. This is not always easy to decide, because if your initial hand is a good one you may be obliged to give him a good card or two. Try to avoid giving him a pair, or a Five. High discards are generally better than low ones. If you are faced with the problem of giving the dealer a Ten or a Five, give him the Ten. Keep pairs and possible runs if you can.

Plan your play carefully. If you don't it is easy to throw points away. Towards the end of the game, watch the score: the player who 'pegs out' first is the winner, even though his opponent might have the better hand.

Study the different scoring combinations, and make sure that you understand just how they are made up.

A great game to play in a pub over a pint, is Five-Card Cribbage.

CASINO
Required: 1 pack of cards, pencil and paper

Once upon a time, in a book on card games, the printer dropped a clanger and misspelt the name of this game as 'cassino'. The error was perpetuated in later books, and today most people think that 'cassino' is right; but I think we will revert to the original and correct spelling.

Casino is a fine game for two people. I remember playing it a very long time ago with my mother; I so well remember the terms 'Big Casino' and 'Little Casino'. The more dignified term is 'Great Casino', but to me it will always be 'Big'.

I say a game for two: it can be adapted for three, but that's not so good; the third player, sandwiched between the first to play and the dealer, is at a disadvantage. And with four players it becomes a partnership game, and rather complicated. So we will just consider two players.

Cut for first deal, lowest card takes the deal, Ace low. After that the winner of each game deals for the next.

All the pip cards have their face value, Ace counting as One; the court cards have no numerical value. The Ten of Diamonds is called Great Casino, and the Two of Spades is Little (or Small) Casino.

You score points at the end of each game according to the cards you have 'taken in'. Great Casino scores 2 points; Little Casino scores 1 point; each Ace scores 1 point; the player who has taken in most cards scores 3 points; the player who has taken in most Spades scores 1 point. In addition, every time a player takes in the last card or all the remaining cards on the table he scores 1 point. This is called a 'sweep'.

The dealer, after the pack has been shuffled and cut, deals two cards face down to his opponent, two face up in the middle of the table, and two face down to himself; then repeats the process, so that each player has four cards and there are four face up on the table.

In turn, beginning with the non-dealer, the players play one card and one only. When they have both played their four cards the dealer deals another four each, and so on until the pack is used up; it is usual for the dealer to draw attention to the fact when he comes to his last deal, in case his opponent hasn't noticed. When the last cards have been played the game is over and each player turns over the cards he has taken in so that the scores can be reckoned up.

So the non-dealer plays first. The object is to take in as many cards as possible, especially scoring cards. There are three things he can do.

He can take in by matching a card from his hand with one or more of the cards on the table. Say there is a Ten on the table and he has a Ten in his hand: he puts his Ten on top of the other, takes them both and places them face down in front of him. If one or the other is Great Casino, so much the better!

If there are two Tens, he can take them both. Or three, for that matter, though it doesn't often happen. Or if there are two or more cards adding up to ten: a Six and a Four, a Nine and an Ace; or a Five, Three, and Two. Or of course he could take one Ten, and a Six and Four.

A court card can only take another of the same value, and only one at a time, however: if he has a King in his hand and there is a King on the table, he can take it; but if there are two Kings he can take only one.

Alternatively, he can 'build'. That means adding a card from his hand to one or more on the table, with the idea of taking them on his next play. Say for example he has a Six and a Two in his hand and there is a Four on the table. He places the Two on the Four and says 'Building Six'. Then on his next play he takes both cards with his Six.

If there happened to be another Six on the table he could take that as well. Of course, you are not allowed to build unless you hold the necessary card with which to take the built-up combination.

You can make more than one build, and take them both in on a single play. For example, say you hold Nine, Two, and Six, and there are a Seven and Three on the table. You could place the Two on the Seven and say 'Building Nine'; then on your next play place the Six on the Three and both on the Seven-Two, saying 'Building Nines'; and on your next play take the lot in with your Nine.

But note that your opponent can take in your build if he has the necessary card. He can also increase your build to suit himself. Say for example you have placed a Two on a Four, as above, with the idea of taking them with your Six on your next play: your opponent can add a Three and say 'Building Nine', and if you don't happen to have a Nine to take it yourself, he snaffles it. If you were lucky enough to have a Ten and an Ace left you could foil him in turn by adding the Ace and saying 'Building Ten'!

There is another kind of building: say you hold two Eights, and there is an Eight on the table. You place one of your Eights on it and say 'Building Eights'. Then next play you take both Eights in with your Eight – and if there happened to be a Six and a Two on the table you could take in those as well.

Now note what you can't do. If one player is, for example, building threes, having placed a Three from his hand on to a Three on the table, and said so, the other player cannot take them with a Six, only with another Three. Nor can he add an Ace to make it a build of Seven, or in any way change the build from what it was originally, one to be taken with a Three and nothing else. And you can only build with a card from your hand, never with a card from the table. For example, there are a Five and a Three on the table: your opponent places a Two on the Five and says 'Building Seven'; you cannot take in the Seven build plus the Three with a Ten.

So much for building, and I hope that I have made it clear. The third alternative play, after taking in and building, is 'trailing', which simply means playing a card from your hand to the middle of the table. If you can't, or at any rate don't, either take in or build, you have to trail.

You must not trail if you have a build on the table waiting to be taken in, or if there is anything else you could take in. For example: on the table are a Five and a Three. You hold a Nine, a Seven, and two Threes. You place one Three on the table Three saying 'Building Threes'. Your opponent trails with a Nine. Now, you could take in the Threes, or the Nine, but you must not trail with your Seven in the hope, shall we say, that his next trail may be a Two.

But if you had not had your build waiting to be take in, you could have trailed with your Seven if you thought it better to do so rather than take in the Nine. That clear?

After both players have played their last cards, any cards left on the table are taken by the player who was last to take in: but this does not count as a sweep, which, you will remember, is clearing the table during earlier play and earns the player 1 point. Sweeps are usually indicated by turning one of the sweep-

32

ing player's cards face up, as a reminder when it comes to the scoring.

So both players turn their taken-in cards face up, and their scores are reckoned up. If each player has 26 cards, neither scores anything for 'cards'. In this case a tie is possible, for apart from sweeps there are 11 points to be won, and if no one gets the 3 for most cards that leaves 8, which might be 4 each.

A point about sweeps, which though obvious ought perhaps to be mentioned: after a sweep the next player has no option but to trail.

When playing for money, some players play 'eleven up'; that is, the first player to reach 11 points is the winner. He receives so many units, pennies or whatever, as indicated by the difference between his score and the loser's. But if he reaches 11 points in only two games, the loser's score is subtracted from twice the winner's; and if the game is won on a single hand, from four times the winner's.

So if A wins the first game 6–5, and the second is drawn 4–4, and B wins the third 10–1; then B wins by 19–11 and receives 8 units. If A wins two games 7–5, 7–5, he receives twice 4 (or 8) units again. But if he wins in one game 11–2 he receives four times 9 (or 36) units.

Lastly: if you like the version of Casino I have explained, you may want to try Royal Casino which is even more absorbing. In this game the court cards have numerical values, Jack 11, Queen 12, and King 13; and an Ace counts as either 1 or 14 as the player wishes. And you can take in more than two court cards. Otherwise the game is played on the same lines, but usually '21 up'.

I haven't said anything about the strategy of the game. Really it's pretty obvious after you have played a few games. And though my explanation may seem a bit lengthy, Casino is actually a straightforward and easy game to learn. I'm sure you will like it.

SOLOMON
Required: 1 pack of cards

A brainteasing game for two.

If you are a Poker player, or if, since you acquired this book, you have begun to understand the game of Poker, this is a fine time-passing variation for you and the other fellow when you are sitting around with nothing else to do. But please read the section on Poker (*see* p 96) before you try it.

You cut for deal, highest card cut taking the deal, and the deal changing hands after each game.

Assuming that I deal first, I peel ten cards off the shuffled pack face up on to the table. Having done this I hand the pack to you.

You consider the ten cards on the table. They would make two poker hands, and you regard them in this light. Then you remove the top six cards from the pack, and without letting me see them, mentally associate them with the cards on the table. Then you arrange them in order according to your strategy.

Now you divide the cards on the table into two separate Poker hands of five cards each. In a moment I shall be allowed to choose one of these two hands, leaving you with the other. I shall be able to discard any number of cards that I think fit, and draw the same number from the pack – from those six cards that you have arranged. So with Solomon-like judgement, you have prepared for me to choose either hand, with as much foresight as possible, and to discard and draw, and still leave you – after you too have discarded and drawn – with the better hand of the two. Do I make it clear?

You know, for example, that if I play correctly I shall choose what looks like the most promising of the two hands, discard three, and draw the top three cards from the pack. And these you have arranged so as to give me the worst possible advantage. If on the other hand I should select the other five cards, discard two and draw two, it would still leave me with the worst hand.

But perhaps I shall guess what you are up to, so I choose the less inviting hand – and ruin your feeble little plan by discarding only one card and drawing one; this will ruin your own discard and wreck the plans you made for a hand to beat mine.

When all the mental jousting is over, the hands are laid down face up and the best hand (according to the rules of Poker) wins.

As you will realize, this is a game of wits, and there is more to it than meets the eye. If all goes well, your plan succeeds and you will win – or was I too clever for you?

Turn by turn you bisect the baby, attempting to outwit the other fellow.

There are so many stratagems you can adopt. If you can pick up a hand which has winning points already, don't discard at all, and therefore don't draw; this may throw a spanner into the works. And yet – this may be just what your opponent planned for, and you are doomed! Try discarding all five cards and drawing five: this might win the game for you.

As you can see, the possibilities are endless, and this makes for a good game. But no betting, please: Solomon is just for fun.

PISHTI ('COOKED')

Required: 1 pack of cards, pencil and paper

This is an excellent game for two people – or four playing as partners. You will notice that it is very like the Dry Game on page 92; in fact, I would imagine that Pishti is the original game.

Pishti, literally translated from the Turkish, means 'cooked'. I was fortunate to have an opportunity of playing the game for several evenings running with Attila Dogan, a chemist in Ankara. It is a game played everywhere in Turkey, where card games are sometimes the only form of entertainment. Attila Dogan, I found, knew some twenty card games intimately.

But let's explain Pishti while it is fresh in my mind. Cut for deal: highest card cut indicates the dealer.

Suppose that you and I are playing and I am to deal. I shuffle the pack and pass it to you: you cut the pack, remove the card at the bottom of the cut-off portion and place it face up on the table, and partly cover it (just so that the index is visible) with the remainder of the cut-off portion.

This exposed card plays a small part in the game; should it be a Jack, you can take it and place it face down in front of you.

I pick up the rest of the pack and deal four cards to you, four to myself, and four in a pile in the middle of the table, turning the last of these face up on top of the others. If this is a Jack then I as dealer take it and replace it with the next card from the pack.

We pick up our cards and look at them, and play begins: but first let us consider the scoring. Jacks are like trumps, and can take any other card. The Two of Clubs, among your cards at the end of the game, scores 2 points; the Ten of Diamonds, 3 points; each Jack and Ace, 1 point; the player who finishes up with most cards scores 3 points. And a Pishti, which I'll explain in a moment, is worth 10 points. The suits of the cards don't enter into the game at all.

So to the play. I dealt, so you go first. If you have a card of the same value as that face-up card on top of the pile in the middle of the table, you play it, and take the lot, putting them and the card you played face down in front of you. Suppose the face-up card is a King; you take the lot with any other King. If you have no King, but you have a Jack, you can still take the lot: a Jack takes anything, remember. But you may prefer to keep your Jack until there is a bigger pile to take.

Before you place the pile you take face down in front of you, have a quick look at the face-down cards to see what they are: it is important to try to remember all the cards that have gone. Suppose at one stage of the game you have two Sixes in your hand and you remember that the other two have gone; you can safely play a Six knowing that I can't take it, except with a Jack.

If you cannot take the pile, then you play on to it, face up, any card which you hope I will not be able to match. So we play in turn, and every time our four cards have been played I deal again, until the pack is used up. Then we have a fresh deal and it's your turn to deal.

When either of us take the pile and the middle of the table is left empty, then of course the other has to play a card face up on to the bare table. This is where Pishti comes in. Say you play an Eight in these circumstances – it only applies when there is only the one card on the table – and I can match it with another Eight, then I play my Eight on to yours, say Pishti, take the two cards and score 10 points. This can happen many times during a game, or not at all.

Then of course you play another card, and so on.

The fun is enhanced by the novel method of keeping the score. You decide beforehand whether you are going to play 101 up or 151 up – that is, the player who first reaches the agreed total is the winner.

You need pencil and paper to keep score. Draw a vertical line to make two columns headed 'I' and 'You' and a horizontal line, as in Bridge, for scoring above and below. At the end of each complete deal the player with the smallest heap of cards can add up his score and subtract his total from 16; the remainder will be the other player's score. These figures are entered below the line.

But Pishtis are scored as they are made, and indicated by a short vertical stroke above the line. Each of these of course indicates 10. In addition, each complete 10 below the line is transferred above, again by means of a short vertical stroke by the side of any Pishti strokes. The odd score above 10 remains below the line as a single digit.

When you have four 10 strokes above the line, the next 10

scored is indicated by crossing the four by a horizontal line, thus indicating 50. To make it clear you can also draw a ring round the 50 symbol. This makes the scoring easy and saves adding up: you can see at a glance when a player reaches 101, or 151, whichever you are aiming at.

To make it clear: suppose in the first deal you and I have scored 8 points each, and you have made three Pishtis. Then below the line goes a figure 8 on each side, while on your side above the line go three strokes.

Next deal: you score 5 points and a Pishti. The 8 already below the line, plus 5, makes 13: cross out the 8, put down a 3, and transfer the balance of 10 above the line by means of a stroke. That's four strokes; cross them through to indicate 10 for your Pishti, and there's a complete 50.

I scored 11 below the line, and two Pishtis. The 11 and the 8 I had before is 19; cross out the 8 and write 9; a stroke above the line for the other 10, and two more strokes for my Pishtis.

The figures below the line are always single digits, above the line are complete fifties and the odd tens.

So it's easy to see at a glance that at this stage your total is 53, and mine 39. And, as I have said, it's easy to see when either of us reaches 101, or 151. Got the idea?

Pishti is an easily learnt, really delightful game. You need considerable skill in remembering cards that have been played, and judging just when to use one of those Jacks.

A variation of the game is Bluff Pishti. It's the same, except that you place your matching card face down on the single card on the table and say Pishti – and if you are bluffing, it isn't a matching card after all. If it is unchallenged by your opponent and you get away with it you score the Pishti. If you are challenged and you were bluffing, you lose the cards and your opponent marks up 20. But if you are challenged and the card did match, and you weren't bluffing, then *you* mark up 20. A very good variation which adds much excitement.

So Pishti to you!

*Games for four
and for all the family*

WHIST

Required: 1 or 2 packs of cards, cribbage-board
(or pencil and paper)

Whist is the grandfather of Contract Bridge – or should I say the grandmother? Who hasn't heard of Whist drives, or taken part in one?

It is a simple matter to learn the rudiments, but the longer you play Whist the more you realize how carefully you must play. And the great secret of good Whist is to remember every card played.

This is a game for four players. You can arrange partners, or cut for partners. Cut for deal, too, Ace counting low in this instance; lowest card deals. Partners sit opposite to one another.

The dealer deals the cards one at a time clockwise, starting with the player on his left, until they each have thirteen cards. The trump suit is decided by turning up the last card dealt; or if you have a second pack it can be cut for trumps, so that the exposing of the last card does not embarrass the holder. Or, of course, with one pack in use, it can be cut for trumps before the deal starts.

In the game of Whist there are thirteen tricks; so after a side has taken six tricks, any acquired above that number are scoring tricks.

The player on the dealer's left leads, i.e. plays first. The others play a card in turn, and must follow suit if they can; if a player cannot follow suit he can play a trump, or throw away a card of one of the other two suits. Failure to follow suit when possible is called revoking, and incurs a penalty of the loss of three tricks.

The winner of each trick leads for the next round.

It is usually a good plan to return your partner's lead.

An old axiom is that the third player plays high. This does not apply, of course, if you can see that your partner has played the winning card; or if you are holding all the master cards, in which case you play the lowest of them. Your partner will then know that you hold the others.

There is another occasion when you do not follow the 'third player plays high' rule, and that is when you finesse. Suppose that your partner leads a low Spade, and the player on your right follows suit. You hold the Ace, Queen, and Jack. You do not know who holds the King, so you finesse with the Queen. If you play your Ace according to the rule, and the King does not fall, then you won't know the fate of your Queen should you lead it next. If, however, you play the Queen, the player on your left must take it with the King if he has it, and then you will know that your Jack is good. There is the possibility of course that the next player may not play the King; then you can assume that either your partner or the player on your right has it.

It could be that the player on your left had the King after all and threw away a small card for some reason – but sticking to it isn't likely to do him any good. Suppose your partner led his only Spade and has a trump ready for that King? If your Queen takes the trick, all well and good; now you lead your Ace, returning your partner's lead. You might collect the opponents' King this time.

This was a speculative finesse.

Let's see what happens the other way round. You lead a small card of a suit of which you hold King, Ten, Eight and Four. Your partner comes up with the Queen and takes the trick. So it is unlikely that the opponent on your right holds the Ace. Your partner now returns your lead with a low card, which indicates that he does not hold the Ace; now you know the worst: that the player on your left has it.

He may have the Jack too. (If your partner had held it, he would have played it in place of the Queen). So you play your Ten; it's an even chance that this will draw the Ace, and then your King will be good. But if he does have the Jack it's just bad luck; anyhow you tried.

This is an obligatory finesse.

Any good Whist-player will tell you that if you 'stick to the rules' you will play good Whist and never let your partner down. These rules look formidable but are really just common sense.

For various combinations of cards in his hand the first player will lead as follows (let's take the trump suit first):

Holding Ace, King, Queen, Jack: lead the Jack. Then your opponents don't know where the other masters are but your partner does. Follow with the Queen.

Holding Ace, King, Queen: for the same reason lead the Queen first, then the King.

41

Holding Ace, King and five others: lead the King, followed by the Ace. But if you have fewer than five others, lead the fourth best.

Now other suits, not trumps:

Holding Ace, King, Queen, Jack (all the masters): lead the King, then the Jack.

Holding Ace, King, Queen: lead the King, then the Queen.

Holding Ace, King, and others: lead the King, then the Ace.

Holding King, Queen, Jack, and one low card: lead the King, then the Jack.

Holding King, Queen, Jack, and more than one low card: lead the Jack, and if you hold five cards, follow with the King; if more than five, the Queen.

Holding Ace and four or more low cards: lead the Ace, followed by the fourth best of those left.

Holding King, Queen, and others: lead the King, and, if this wins, lead the fourth best of those left.

Holding Ace, Queen, and Jack with or without a low card: lead the Ace, then the Queen. But, it is, of course, better not to lead from this combination at all if you can help it; if the lead comes to you you can finesse and have a chance of making all three high cards.

If these rules are adhered to, you will discover that in most instances they almost automatically make the cards you hold into winners.

Now the second player: he plays very differently.

Holding Ace, King, Queen, with a low card led: play the Queen.

Holding Ace, King, Jack, with a low card led: play the King.

Holding Ace, King, and others, with a low card led: play the King.

Holding Ace, Queen, Ten and others, if a low trump is led: play the Ten. Or if the Jack is led, play the Ace.

Holding Ace, Queen, and others, or Ace, Jack, Ten, and others, with a low card led: play low; but in the latter case if the suit is trumps, play the Ten.

Holding Ace and low cards, with a low card led: play low.

Holding King, Queen, Jack, and others, with a low card led: play the Jack.

Holding King, Queen, and others, with a low card led: play the Queen.

Holding Queen, Jack, Ten, and others, with a low card led: play the Queen.

Holding Queen, Jack and others, with a low card led: play the Jack.

Holding Ace and others, with the Queen led: play the Ace.

Holding King and others, with a low card led: play low.

Holding King and one low card, or Queen and one low card, with a low card led: play low.

But with Queen and one low card and the Jack or Ten led, play the Queen.

The object of all this is to force the third player to play as high a card as possible.

Now for the third player. The general rule is that he plays high, with the following exceptions:

(1) When he does not hold a card higher in value than the two just played, he naturally plays his lowest.

(2) When he holds all the master cards, he plays his lowest master.

(3) And, when a finesse is desirable.

As for the fourth player: it is his business to try to win the trick. But if it has already been won by his partner, then he discards; that is, he throws away a useless card, e.g. a low card of a long suit if he cannot follow suit, otherwise his lowest card in the suit led.

But note this in the case of his being unable to follow suit: if he holds only one or two of another suit, and they are useless cards, it may be a good plan to throw them away with a view to trumping that suit later.

Now for a few things to remember in order to play good Whist.

Always lead from your strongest suit; your partner, if playing correctly, will do the same.

Study the cards played by your partner and your opponents. In this way, by comparing the play with the cards in your own hand, you can get an approximate idea of the lie of the cards and the value of your own and your partner's hands.

In Whist your strongest suit is usually your longest. A long suit will break many an opponent's heart.

How to lead? Suppose that your strongest suit has the Ace but not the King. Lead the Ace. Your partner should know that you do not have the King and want to make the Ace while you can.

Next you will lead a low card, from the same suit, hoping that your partner holds the King. If he doesn't, you will lose the trick. But if the King is played, as it should be, it will make good a Queen held by you or your partner, to be played later when you regain the lead.

If you hold, say, the Ace, King, Queen, and others, lead with your Queen. If it is not trumped by your opponents, your partner will know that you hold the master cards.

If when it is your lead you have a singleton, i.e. only one card of a suit, not trumps, whatever its value, lead it. Your partner may win the trick, but even if he doesn't he now knows that you would like him to return the lead in that suit. You will then be able to trump, and your partner will no doubt realize this.

When returning your partner's lead there are one or two things to remember. It is not always necessary for you to return the lead at once; you may ruin your own hand by doing so. So play what you want to play, and come back to his suit later. Your partner, realizing what you are up to, will help you out with your play.

If your partner leads with a low card in a suit of which you have Ace, Jack, and one other, take the trick with the Ace, then lead the Jack. Your partner will know that you are doing your best in that suit. If you hold the Ace, Jack, and three others, return the lead with your lowest card; save the Jack because the play of the cards could make it the master.

By leading correctly you are in fact conveying information to your partner all the time. Lead properly and remember the cards played, and you will make a good Whist-player.

There are one or two rules about discarding. If the lead is not in trumps, discard the lowest of your weakest suit. If your partner has led trumps and you can't follow suit, again discard the lowest of your weakest suit. But when your opponents lead trumps and you can't follow suit, discard the lowest card of your strongest suit. These are two rules you must remember.

If your opponents keep the lead and continue to take tricks, and you are unable to follow suit, you must use your head about discarding. The whole result will depend on your judgement; make sure that you keep cards of value.

Possibly, when you become more expert you will sometimes discard a higher card than necessary, thus giving your opponents the idea that it is the last card you have of the suit and will be trumping next round; this sometimes pays off. With experience you will soon feel your way.

About the meaning of trumps and their use: the suit which is trumps (and this applies to all games in which trumps are used) is the most powerful. The Two of trumps beats the Ace of any other suit.

If you find that you have numerically strong trumps it may be advisable to lead them and draw trumps; then you and your partner will be able to cash in on long suits without fear of being trumped by the opponents.

If you are numerically short of trumps they must be played carefully, and perhaps with your partner's help you may be able to 'cross trump'. This situation arises when you both have short or void suits. You discover in the course of play that your partner has no Diamonds, and your partner knows that you want a return lead in Clubs; in fact you have no more. Your partner leads a Club and you trump it; you lead a Diamond which he trumps. So you both make your low trumps, one by one, to the chagrin of your opponents who are forced to discard valuable cards.

When you play Whist, play silently. That maxim was the origin of the name. Think about every card you play. Do not let your partner down, and he will probably treat you in the same way.

Finally: scoring. Scoring is by tricks and honours. Every trick after the first six counts. If you and your partner just scrape home, taking seven tricks while your opponents take six, you have won by the odd trick; if you take eight while they take five, you score two by tricks, and so on. Honours are the Ace, King, Queen, and Jack of the trump suit; if you and your partner initially hold all four between you, you score four; if you hold any three, you score two. If you and your partner hold two and your opponents the other two, honours are divided and no one scores.

A score of five tricks and/or honours constitutes a game. Its value in points varies according to what the opponents have scored. If they have scored three or four, the game is a 'single' worth 1 point; if they have scored one or two, it is a 'double' worth 2 points; if they have not scored at all the game is a 'treble' worth 3 points.

The best of three games constitutes a rubber, and the winners

45

of the rubber get 2 extra points. If a side wins the first two games of the rubber, the third game is not played.

It is usual to settle up after each rubber at an agreed amount per point. each member of a partnership settling with one opponent. The value in points of a rubber can vary from 1 to 8. Say one pair have won two singles, but the other pair have won a treble. The first pair have $1 + 1 + 2$ for the rubber, total 4; from that is deducted 3, the value of the second pair's treble. Net pay-out, one unit. If on the other hand the first pair have won two trebles and the other pair nothing: the pay-out is 8 units, i.e. $3+3+2$ for the rubber.

There are many more rules connected with formal Whist, but those outlined above will be enough to go along with.

At the start I mentioned Whist drives. If you have the chance of taking part in one, do: you will have a lot of fun, even though you play badly. The better players will have fun anyway. But you will be won over for all time.

You will be given a card which tells you the number of the table at which you start. There are spaces for the numbers of all the tables at which you play, also for your (and your partner's) score at each table; to guard against cheating an opponent enters and initials your score, and you do the same on his or her card. Scoring is very simple: it's just the total tricks won by you and your partner.

Partners are changing all the time. After each hand, the winning lady moves to the next higher table, the winning man to the next lower, the losing lady stays where she is and the losing man moves one place to the left at the same table.

Trumps for each hand are fixed, either by being indicated in rotation on your score-card. or indicated on the table, or called out before each hand. A bell generally tells you all when to move on. Sometimes there are 'novelties,' like a hand of No Trumps, or one in which your score is the number of tricks your opponents have made – in which case, of course, you try to lose tricks.

At the end there are prizes for ladies and men with the highest totals, sometimes 'booby' prizes for lowest scores, sometimes prizes for 'hidden numbers', i.e. a certain score not disclosed until the end.

As I say, it's a lot of fun.

SOLO WHIST

Required: 1 pack of cards, counters (or matches) for stakes

Solo Whist is for me the best of all card games. It is so varied, and, although it needs as much skill as Contract Bridge, I think that a better time can be had by all at Solo – but, of course, this is only my opinion.

Solo Whist is a game for four players. You need a pack of cards without jokers; you don't need pencil and paper because you pay as you go.

You agree on a unit stake beforehand, however small; it spoils the game to play for love because with nothing to lose people tend to bid recklessly. Before decimalization we used to speak of 'Twopenny Solo', 'Sixpenny Solo' and so on, that being the value of the unit, which must be divisible by four. So make it two new pence, or four, or whatever you decide; you can, of course, make the unit four counters or matches and cash them at the agreed rate afterwards.

Solo Whist is possibly the most-played card game in Great Britain. You cut for deal, and the player with the lowest card deals. The pack is shuffled, and cut by the player on the dealer's right. The dealer now proceeds to deal three cards at a time round the table, starting with the player on his left, face downwards; four rounds and a final round of single cards, the last card (the dealer's) being turned face up to indicate the trump suit. After each game the player to the left of the previous dealer takes the deal, shuffling lightly or merely cutting the pack before dealing.

Having picked up their cards and sorted them into suits (always in the order, Hearts – Clubs – Diamonds – Spades) the players consider in which of six different ways the game will be played. Suppose, however, all players pass; the cards are thrown in, reshuffled, and dealt afresh by the next dealer, and usually each player contributes a small, previously agreed amount to a 'kitty'. The kitty is picked up by the next player to win a game – excluding 'Prop and cop', which I will describe.

Suppose on the next deal the first player passes. The second thinks that with the help of another player they could make eight tricks. So he calls 'Prop', meaning 'I propose (a partnership)'. Another player decides to go in with him, so he says 'Cop', meaning 'I accept.' The first player to call (the one on the

47

dealer's left) may cop even though he had already passed; no other player who has passed may do so.

So the game begins, as long as no one has overbid the prop-and-cop call. In every game the player on the dealer's left leads, except when the bid is an *'abondance déclarée'*, as you will see.

If the partners make their eight tricks each receives one unit from one opponent – that is, the 'prop' player settles with one opponent and the 'cop' chap with the other – plus $\frac{1}{4}$ unit for each trick made over the eight. If they fail to make the eight tricks, they pay out one unit plus $\frac{1}{4}$ unit for each trick lost over six. So, for example, if they make ten tricks they collect $1 + \frac{1}{4} + \frac{1}{4} = 1\frac{1}{2}$ units; if they make only five and lose eight they pay out $1 + \frac{1}{4} + \frac{1}{4} = 1\frac{1}{2}$ units.

Prop and cop is the least important of the calls. Next highest is solo. This means that the player who calls has undertaken to make five tricks off his own bat – not as easy as it may sound. If he wins, he receives from each of the other three players one unit plus $\frac{1}{4}$ unit for each trick made over five. If he loses he pays each of them 1 unit plus $\frac{1}{4}$ unit for each trick lost over five.

Next highest bid is *misère*. This call means that the player will attempt to lose all thirteen tricks. There are no trumps in *misère*. If the caller succeeds, he receives two units from each of the other players; if he takes a trick, he pays them two units each. He cannot take more than one trick because as soon as he is forced to take one the game is over.

Abondance (it's incorrect to call it 'abundance') is the next highest bid. If you make this call you intimate that you are prepared to make, alone and unaided, nine tricks; but you can name your own trump suit. You do not name it until you have gained the call and play is about to begin; if you did so and were overcalled, the information would be useful to the other players or perhaps prejudicial to the overcall. There is one exception to this rule: *abondance* can be overcalled by *abondance* in trumps, and everyone knows what the trump suit is.

If successful you receive three units from each player and $\frac{1}{2}$ unit for each overtrick; if you lose, you pay out three units to each player plus $\frac{1}{2}$ unit for each trick lost over five. So do not make this call lightly. The pay-out is the same for the *abondance* in trumps.

Next highest bid is *misère ouverte*, a very exciting call which happens only once in a while. As with *misère* you undertake to lose all the tricks, but there is one important difference: after the first trick has been taken you lay down your cards face upwards so that the other players can see what you hold. And you hope for the best. If you win you receive four units from each player; if you lose you pay them four each, so it will cost you 12 units. So be very wary!

Abondance déclarée is the highest call. If you make this call (and it will happen only occasionally), you undertake to make all thirteen tricks. There will be no trumps, and the caller himself makes the first lead. In most cases the hand is so good that the caller can just lay down, because it is unbeatable. If you win, you receive six units from each player. And if you lose you may as well go out of business; it costs you 18 units, six to each.

A word about bidding. The first player may call a cautious 'Prop'. No other player takes him up on this; so he can in effect overbid himself and call 'Solo'. This must carry because no player who has passed can bid, with the exception already noted – that the first caller can cop.

Again: suppose the first player calls solo. The second over-calls him with *misère*. Third calls *abondance* – presumably, in view of the previous solo call, intending to make a different suit trumps from that of the turned-up card. Fourth player passes; so does the first player on the second time round. Second player now decides to take a chance and make it *misère ouverte*. Not to be outdone the third player increases his call to *abondance déclarée*, and of course this carries. This example of over-bidding is an extreme one: but it can happen, especially if there have been several passes all round on the previous deals and a tempting kitty has been built up.

Now, all this may sound very complicated. But of all the card games, Solo is the one you learn most easily. You can play it almost at once; but naturally you only become an expert player over the years.

The great thing is to assess the value of your hand. Personally, I never like to play prop and cop; but this is of course entirely up to you if you want to win the odd unit or two.

Having been dealt your hand, you have a look at it. First of all you look for a possible solo, five certain or likely tricks. Four Aces and a King would be almost a certainty – but there is always the possibility of weird hands against you and freak trumping.

49

Ace, King, Queen and a couple more trumps should see you through, especially if you are short on another suit; or perhaps you have eight smaller trumps and feel that you should make five or six of them. Yes, solo is easy enough; just look for five near-certain tricks.

Misère must be carefully considered. Here you need a lot of luck. Clever players may catch you out. Your lowest cards in the four suits may be Two, Two, Two, and Five. You feel so safe. But a hundred to one those other fellows may play a two and a four – and the third has none of that suit and throws away – and you have to take the trick with your five!

So consider that hand of yours carefully. If you have a doubt about a suit with too many high cards in it, unless you have the low ones too, just do not take the chance. But a void suit, i.e. one in which you have nothing, can help: if, say, you have no Hearts and a low Heart is led, it's lovely to be able to throw away your dangerous Ace of Spades! But if you take a chance on an impossible *misère* hand and lose, the other players have a right to feel annoyed because you may have stopped someone from making a certain solo. So you must genuinely feel that you can make it.

Abondance: if you decide on this call you must be reasonably sure that you can make nine tricks with the other three against you. Look over your hand and make sure that you can see nine tricks before you plunge.

Misère ouverte: here I can say only that you must be able to see little likelihood of being forced to take a trick. After some experience you will get a feeling about this: you will know what chances you can take, and with that little bit of luck you can lay them down.

Abondance déclarée: here there is not much of a game to play as a rule. The simple reason is that more often than not you are holding a freak hand which cannot be beaten; your luck is in; and you collect.

There are occasions of course when with sheer good play and a bit of luck as well you can pull off a risky *abondance déclarée,* but I am afraid that I have not the ability to put into words just how you would assess a hand for this possibility.

Solo Whist is a fine game. Next time you have a chance of making a fourth on a long train journey, join in – but beware of sharpers and make sure the stakes are not too high.

CONTRACT BRIDGE

Required: 1 bridge set (or 2 packs of cards), 1 set of scoring-tables, 1 scoring-pad (or paper) and pencil.

I think that one could safely describe Contract Bridge as the number one of all card games. Whist was its ancestor; from Whist came Bridge in which the dealer nominated the trump suit and played his partner's hand, disclosed, as the 'dummy'; then came Auction Bridge, with bidding to decide the trump suit; and finally, about 1926, Contract Bridge, in which the important feature is that to gain maximum benefit a partnership must bid up to the full capability of their combined hands.

Playing occasionally one can never reach perfection, but with players around the same level it can still be a lot of fun; woe betide the unfortunate beginner who joins a bunch of experts and proceeds to spoil their game!

So let's consider what we may call the family game, for people who play together occasionally. If you get really hooked then there is a wealth of literature on Contract Bridge available to you in bookshops and libraries, and then you can take this fascinating game really seriously.

If you happen to have a friend or relative who is an expert and you can persuade him to take you through a few rubbers stage by stage, explaining everything as you go, that's fine: but I am assuming that no such situation exists and you have to start from scratch.

You will need two 52-card packs without Jokers; what is called a Bridge set, two matching packs with differently coloured backs, is best. With a set you usually get a couple of scoring-tables (*see* p 60), so keep one by you until you can memorize all the scoring. (Some experienced players never manage to get it all off by heart!)

And buy some scoring-pads: you can, of course, use plain paper, but ruled pads are cheap enough and save trouble. A folding baize-topped card-table is the most convenient to play on, but you can use any old table.

Contract Bridge (familiarly known as either Bridge or Contract) is essentially a game for four players; there are variations for two or three players, but they are inferior to the real thing and we needn't concern ourselves with them.

Before we go any further, let's learn the relative value of the

51

suits. Clubs rank lowest; then Diamonds; Hearts rank higher still; and Spades highest of the four. And in bidding, No Trumps overcalls a suit bid.

I don't suppose I need to explain that in Contract Bridge as in other games which involve trumps, even the lowest trump card beats even the highest card of another suit. So if your opponent has played, say, the Ace of Hearts, and you have no Hearts and cannot follow suit, you can, if Clubs are trumps, take the Ace, and the trick, with your Two of Clubs. Mind you, if your other opponent, the next player, has no Hearts either he can over-trump you with the Three of Clubs and you would lose the trick after all.

And, of course, as in most other card games, you must follow suit if possible. If Hearts are led, you must play a Heart if you have one. If you break this rule you have 'revoked', and you are branded as a careless player. If the revoke is discovered right away, before the lead has been made to the next trick, then a correct card is substituted for the revoke card, and the latter becomes a penalty card: it is laid face up on the table and must be played at the first opportunity. If the revoke is discovered later, the trick containing it goes to the opponents of the re-voker, unless it is already theirs; also the next trick won by the offending side. If the trick containing the revoke was taken by the non-offending side, then the next two tricks won by the revoking side are transferred to the opponents, if there are two. If there is only one, then that is transferred. But a revoke in the twelfth trick carries no penalty.

So be careful. If you cannot follow suit, you either trump, or throw away a card of another suit.

Spread the pack face down on the table and draw for part-ners. The two players who draw the highest cards (Ace is high) are partners against the two who draw the lowest, and the player who draws the highest card is the dealer. If two players should both draw cards of the same value, say the Tens of Heart and Spades, remember the relative value of the suits: the Ten of Spades ranks as the higher.

Partners sit opposite to one another. It is usual for the player on the dealer's left to shuffle the pack, and for the player on the dealer's right to cut it: that is, to lift off anything from a quarter to three-quarters of the pack and put it on the dealer's side of the balance. The dealer then completes the cut by placing the balance on to the cut-off portion, and proceeds to deal the cards singly, clockwise round the table, beginning with the player on his left. It is customary, while he is dealing, for his partner to shuffle the other pack and then place it on his right ready for the next game.

When the deal is over, each player picks up his thirteen cards, and advisedly, arranges them in suits; in order, preferably. The last card dealt should of course fall to the dealer – if it doesn't, either he has misdealt or there are one or more cards missing from the pack!

Now the players study their hands and assess their value. Obviously, you look for high cards; you also weigh up the length of the suits. The average distribution of the suits is 4, 3, 3, 3; for example, you might hold four Spades, three Hearts, three Diamonds, and three Clubs. Now, if you found you held six Spades, three Hearts, three Diamonds, and only one Club, you would think to yourself: 'It will be fine for me if Spades are trumps. The other three players have only seven between them, and my partner may hold three of those; and, if my opponents have strong Clubs, I could trump those the second time round.'

So – Spades might be your bid, especially if you hold some of the high Spades, and a good card or two in Hearts and Diamonds as well.

Very simple, that's the line of thought. If you hold high cards in all four suits, then No Trumps might be your first thought. There's more to it than this, of course: skilled bidding gives the maximum information to your partner, so that the two of you can arrive at the contract which will earn you the highest possible number of points – or conversely, enable you to defeat your opponent's contract if possible.

Assessing your own hand, and getting an insight into the hands held by your partner and your opponents, is a matter of what is known as 'card sense'. This – desirable in all card games, but never more than in Contract Bridge – is something you can acquire only by experience. And between ourselves, some devoted card-players never seem to acquire it! So rule-of-thumb systems have been devised from time to time, to help the beginner – and those without much card sense. Here is a 'points system' which may serve as a rough guide until you find that you can dispense with it:

Reckon an Ace as 4 points, a King as 3, a Queen 2, a Jack 1. If you have a 'void suit', in other words none at all of a suit, reckon that as 3 points; a 'singleton', i.e. only one card of a suit, 2 points; a 'doubleton' (only two cards of a suit), 1 point.

Remember that the total points value of the top four cards in all the four hands is 40, and you will see that on the face of it a hand adding up to 10 points is nothing to shout about! If you can see 20 points in your hand, however, then it is a strong one. But I think that you would know that from your own common sense, don't you? And there are snags in such a system which you will soon spot: for example, it is obviously better to hold the Ace, King, and Queen of one suit than of three different suits – yet the 'points value' is the same in both cases.

There is another, rather more sensible system, of hand-valuation called Honour Tricks. It's perhaps too complicated to explain here: so use the points system at first if it helps you, reckoning that you need a points value of at least 12 or 13 to make an opening bid. But better still, *think* about your hand and its possibilities in combination with that of your partner, and the more experience you gain from actual play, the better you will be able to evaluate it.

So let us consider the bidding, the first and perhaps the most important part of the game. Almost as important is the ability to remember what bids have been made previously, during the play, and to remember what cards have gone. An expert Contract Bridge player, such as my old friend the late Jack Salvin, a member of the Magic Circle, will tell you that if the players bid correctly he can almost certainly foretell the result of a game before the cards are played. Incidentally, Jack Salvin never arranged the cards in his hand – but he was an expert; I advise you to do so.

Now, the bidding is just like an auction. One Spade outbids One Diamond; Two Diamonds outbids One Spade. Two No Trumps outbids Two Hearts. It is not essential to open the bidding with a bid of One; say you held strong Diamonds in good length, six or seven of them headed by the Ace, King, and Queen, and no Spades at all, you might open with Three Diamonds with the idea that if your opponents held the Spades evenly divided neither would venture to mention them. This is known as a 'pre-emptive' bid. (If it should be your partner who holds the Spades after all, don't worry: you could throw away useless cards on his winning Spades and be able to do some useful trumping.)

Similarly, you don't have to overbid by the bare margin: when advisable you can overcall One Heart with Two Spades, where One would suffice, or Two Spades with Three, not Two, No Trumps.

Bidding goes numerically, and takes no account of scoring values. As you will see presently when we consider the scoring, a successful bid of Three No Trumps scores 100 points, while Four Clubs bid and made earns you only 80 points – nevertheless, Four Clubs overcalls Three No Trumps.

Now, what does the bidding mean, and what is its object?

There are thirteen tricks in a hand. So a bare win means that one side has taken seven tricks and the other side six. The winners have won by a margin of one trick. Hence, it's the tricks over six that count. So to bid One Spade means, in effect, that the bidder considers that if Spades are trumps, and he has average support from his partner, he can take seven tricks – one over the six.

Suppose that as the bidding stands, one opponent has called Two Hearts. Your partner overcalls with Two Spades, meaning: 'Partner, my Spades are good, and as long as Spades are trumps I'm not too worried about those Hearts; with a bit of support from you I could make eight tricks if Spades are trumps, so how are you fixed?'

But the other opponent overcalls him with Two No Trumps. That implies that he has a 'stopper' in Spades, for example the King and one or two more, to prevent you two from racing away and making Spade tricks before he has a chance to get going; some good Clubs and Diamonds; and relying on his partner's good Hearts, which he has shown he has, he should be able to make eight tricks if there is no trump suit.

You hold, perhaps, four or five small Spades, no Hearts at all, and some useful Clubs and Diamonds. So you raise your partner to Three Spades: and what you mean to tell him is: 'Partner, my hand wouldn't be much use against a No Trump declaration, but if Spades are trumps I can give you quite a lot of help.'

As I have said, the main object of the bidding is to arrive at the best possible contract with the combined hands of yourself and your partner in order to amass winning points. But you gain

55

points, too, if you prevent your opponents from fulfilling their contract. If you consider that they have overreached themselves and you and your partner can stop them from making their Three No Trumps, or whatever it is, you can call 'Double'. This doubles the penalties they incur for failure; but it also brings them a bonus if they succeed after all. If they feel pretty sure that they can succeed despite your challenge one of them may call 'Redouble', and the points for tricks made are doubled again – so are penalties for falling short.

First player to call is the dealer. Then the call passes clockwise round the table. You are not compelled to call (or bid); if you don't think that your hand justifies a bid, or if you want to wait awhile and see how things go, you say 'Pass' or 'No bid'. The fact that you have passed does not debar you from bidding next time round.

It sometimes happens that the cards are very evenly distributed and no player feels that his hand is strong enough to make an opening bid; so everyone calls 'Pass' or 'No bid', the cards are thrown in, and the deal passes to the next player.

Otherwise, the bidding goes round the table until three players say 'No bid' consecutively; then the bidding is over. The player who made the highest bid now has to make his 'contract'. The player to his left leads. The declarer – that is, the player who has the contract – plays both his own and his partner's hands. For this purpose, as soon as the first card has been led, the declarer's partner lays down his hand, sorted into suits, in columns, the cards overlapping so that they can clearly be seen (*see* p 57).

This hand is known as the dummy. Having laid it down, the declarer's partner takes no further part in the play until the contract is either made or defeated; he should not comment, or pick out cards to be played, or even, preferably, gather up the tricks. All he can do is to watch.

There is just one point to make clear: the player who makes the last bid is not necessarily the declarer. If you were, say, the first to bid Spades, and the last bid was made when your partner raised you to Four Spades, then you are the declarer because you initiated the bidding in Spades.

Now we will examine the bidding in an imaginary game. For purposes of illustration it is convenient to designate the players as North, East, South, and West, North and South being part-

ners, and East and West partners: South is the dealer and first to call.

South: 'One Spade.' (His Spades are strong, six of them headed by the Ace, King, and Queen; he has nothing much in Hearts or Diamonds, and he has no Clubs.)

West: 'No bid.' (No suit is strong enough to 'show'.)

North: 'Two Clubs.' (He holds six of them to the King and Jack; Ace and King of Hearts, two Diamonds, and three Spades. He is not arguing against his partner's Spade bid, but he must show those Clubs.)

East: 'Two Diamonds.' (He has six, headed by the King, Queen, Ten, only one small Spade, and as he has the Ace and two more Clubs they are useful in view of the previous player's bid.

South: 'Two Spades.' (Having no Clubs, his partner's call gives him confidence; he may be able to throw away losing Diamonds on his partner's winning Clubs or trump if the opponents beat the losing ones.)

West: 'Three Diamonds.' (Having the Ace, he feels that he is just about strong enough to support his partner's call.)

North: 'Three Spades.' (He holds three, and those Hearts and Clubs as well.)

East: 'Four Diamonds.' (Now that he knows that he can expect some help from his partner, probably the Ace, he bids up, especially as he could trump Spades on the second round.)

South: 'Four Spades.' (Taking a bit of a chance; but nothing venture, nothing win.)

West: 'Double.' (He holds three Spades, and he suspects that South has overreached himself in view of what he now knows of his partner's hand.)

North: 'No bid.' (All he can do; he is not strong enough to redouble, nor to 'take out' into Five Clubs.)

East: 'No bid.' (He has the same feeling about South's hand as his partner.)

South: 'No bid.' (He thinks he has a reasonable chance of making his contract, but he is far from being confident enough to redouble.)

So the play starts. South having the contract, West leads; then North lays down his hand as dummy and retires temporarily from the game.

You will be wondering what cards the four players held, and what was the result. Well, North's hand was illustrated on page 57 when I showed you how to lay out the dummy; and presently we shall play through the whole hand. Before we do that, however, there is a lot to explain about the scoring: so let us have a look at the scoring-table (*see* p 60).

The object of Contract Bridge is to amass points, not only by winning games but also by gaining bonus and penalty points. A game is 100 or more points earned purely by making tricks which you have contracted to make. These are the points shown at the top of the table. You will see that you can make game on a single hand by making a contract of five Clubs or Diamonds ($5 \times 20 = 100$) or four Hearts or Spades ($4 \times 30 = 120$) or three No Trumps ($40+30+30=100$). If your contract is doubled, then three Clubs or Diamonds, or two Hearts or Spades, or two No Trumps makes you a game; if you redouble, then it only needs two Clubs or Diamonds, one Heart or Spade, one No Trump.

58

But if you don't make your contract, what tricks you do make count nothing towards game. And if your contract is for three Spades, for example, and you make five, you score only 90 towards game (3 × 30); the value of the 'overtricks' is a premium score, not a game score.

A rubber is the best of three games. That is, if you make the first game, your opponents the next, and you the third, then you have won that rubber and get a bonus of 500 points. But if you make two games on the trot, the rubber is over and in that case you get 700 points.

If you look at the scoring-pad shown on page 67, you will see that as well as being divided into 'We' and 'They' columns, it is divided into upper and lower halves by a line. Points which count for game are entered 'below the line', and all other points 'above the line'. Suppose that you have made a Three Spades contract, you score 90 below the line. Now you need only a successful One Club contract to bring your game score over the 100 needed; a line is drawn beneath the 90 and 20 and that indicates that you have a game. But if instead of your making the One Club, your opponents bid and make Three No Trumps, 100 points would be entered in their column and the game would be theirs; your 90 would not be lost altogether, but it would not count towards your next game, you would have to start afresh.

As soon as one side or the other has won a rubber, it is best to continue with a fresh sheet of the scoring-pad, though if there is plenty of space left on it you could draw a double line below the games of that rubber.

Back to the scoring-table. You will see a reference to 'Vulnerability'. A partnership which has won one game towards a rubber becomes 'vulnerable'. As you will see from the table, that state brings the penalties for failure to make a contract, especially if you are doubled, up to quite terrifying heights. If you are vulnerable, and your opponents have doubled your call, and you are two tricks short of your contract, they get 500 points, which is as much as they would earn by winning a three-game rubber. As some small compensation, you do at least get 200 points for each overtrick when you are doubled: but possible penalties far outweigh this small advantage.

So when you are vulnerable you are naturally a bit more cautious and conservative in your bidding. It's no good going all

	Odd Tricks Bid and Won in	UNDOUBLED	DOUBLED
TRICK POINTS FOR DECLARER	Clubs or Diamonds, each	20	40
	Hearts or Spades, each	30	60
	No-trump { first	40	80
	{ each subsequent	30	60

Redoubling doubles the doubled points for Odd Tricks.
Vulnerability does not affect points for Odd Tricks.
100 Trick Points constitute a Game.

		NOT VULNERABLE	VULNERABLE
PREMIUM POINTS FOR DEFENDERS | DECLARER	**Overtricks**		
	Undoubled each	Trick Value	Trick Value
	Doubled each	100	200
	Undertricks		
	Undoubled, each	50	100
	Doubled { first	100	200
	{ each subsequent	200	300

Redoubling doubles the doubled points for Overtricks and
　　Undertricks.
Making a double contract: where a doubled (or redoubled)
　　contract is made by the declarer, the declaring side score
　　an additional 50 points.

PREMIUM POINTS FOR DECLARER | HOLDER	**Honours in One Hand**	{ All Honours	150
		{ Four Trump Honours	100
		{ Four Aces at No Trump	150
	Slams Bid and Won	{ Little, not vulnerable, 500; vulnerable	750
		{ Grand „　　„　　1000;　　„	1500
	Rubber Points	{ Two game	700
		{ Three game	500

Unfinished Rubber: The winners of one game score 300
　　points.
Unfinished Game: A part score in an unfinished game carries
　　a bonus of 50 points.
Doubling and Redoubling do not affect points for Honours,
　　Slams, or Rubber.
Vulnerability does not affect points for Honours.

out for games and rubber if in doing so you are going to hand out hundreds of points to the other side.

Next you will see the bonus points for honours. Honours are the Ace, King, Queen, Jack, and Ten of the trump suit, when they are held in one hand. You get 100 points for holding four of the five, or 150 if you hold all five; you also get 150 points for holding all four Aces in one hand on a No Trump call.

And now we come to the really big scoring: points for Slams. A Little Slam is six tricks bid and made; a Grand Slam is seven tricks bid and made, in other words you have taken all the thirteen tricks. As you see from the table, you can earn as many as 1,500 points for a Grand Slam when you are vulnerable, and that's really something: but you have to have the courage to bid it.

Now and again a freak distribution turns up, and you could conceivably get a Grand Slam by the pure luck of the deal: you might be dealt all the Spades, or all the Aces, Kings, and Queens and the odd Jack. In these cases you would call Seven Spades, or Seven No Trumps, and you would have a 'lay-down' hand; no possible defence could prevent you from making the contract. But such manna from heaven does not fall more than once or twice in a lifetime, and for the most part Contract Bridge is a game of skill: even when the cards are favourably distributed between your partner and yourself, it still needs thoughtful and informative bidding to arrive at the right decision.

Just one more point before we leave the scoring-table: those references to unfinished games and rubbers. Those are just for the odd times when play has to be abandoned before the rubber can be completed; you might have to get up from the table with a game in hand and 90 points towards the next, which would be exasperating, so you would score 350 points as some consolation.

Everything else about the scoring should be clear. To the beginner, this table looks pretty formidable. But you don't need to learn it off by heart before you can start to play: have a copy at your side for reference, and that's where those score-pads you get with some Bridge sets come in handy. And if, as I advise, you make a practice of entering the scores on the pad for yourself right from the start, you will be surprised how quickly you master the table. The sooner, the better: for as you will soon realize, your bidding is greatly influenced by the scoring system.

You may, for example, sometimes find that a 'sacrifice bid' is worth while. Suppose that your opponents are vulnerable, and look like bidding a contract which will give them the rubber, while you are not vulnerable. It may be a good plan to bid higher than your and your partner's hands really justify; you may force them to overbid their hands and perhaps incur heavy penalties, while if you are 'left in' with a contract you cannot possibly make, it will cost you only 50 points for each trick by which you fall short, as long as you are not doubled.

But you have to weigh up the pros and cons carefully and sensibly. Even expert players sometimes make silly 'sacrifices' and lose on balance in the long run. So always keep that scoring-table in mind as you bid.

Before we go on to consider the play of the hands, a word about what to play for. If you are playing for money, fix stakes beforehand: £5 a hundred points for millionaires, more likely a penny a hundred for people like you and me. In the Bridge clubs from 5p to 25p a hundred is usual. It's still good fun to play for nothing, though as with other card games, that tends to encourage some players to make rash and extravagant bids, knowing they have nothing to lose; and they spoil the game.

So when you have finished, tot up the 'we' and 'they' columns on the scoring-pads and subtract the smaller from the larger total. Ignore odd fifties or less, and regard 60 to 90 as 100. With evenly-matched players and unless there are a lot of freak hands, even after a long evening's play the difference is usually no more than a thousand points or so. So at a penny a hundred no one is going to go bankrupt – but what joy to find yourself 20p to the good!

Now that the all-important bidding is clear, I hope – and if it isn't don't despair, it will soon come to you – we can consider the play.

In general the play of the cards is similar to that in Whist, to which you can refer if you are not clear: this applies mainly to the defending side, i.e. the side which is attempting to defeat a contract. Principles such as returning one's partner's lead, and finessing, are applicable to Contract Bridge. But remember the vital differences. The declarer plays his partner's hand, the dummy, in conjunction with his own: and the dummy, after the initial lead, is laid on the table for all to see. This fact greatly influences the play, naturally. And of course one's memory of the previous bidding gives one a far better idea of the other players' hands than is ever possible in Whist.

Now we will play through that same game which I used on page 57 to illustrate bidding. I suggest that you set out the cards in front of you and follow the play with me. This is quite a tricky game for the declarer to play. Here are the full hands as dealt (*see* below).

You will remember that South dealt and that he is 'in' with a contract of Four Spades Doubled. West leads the Ace of Diamonds – let's use abbreviations, the AD – and North lays down the dummy.

South studies the dummy carefully in conjunction with his own hand. It is not going to be easy to make his contract. He must draw trumps – he hopes that East and West have two each – because he can't risk having North's winning Clubs trumped; he would like to throw away his losing Diamonds on North's winning Clubs, and trump the opponents' winning Clubs.

South plays the 3D from dummy, East plays the 4D, South the 5D.

	Spades: 10 7 6	
	Hearts: A K	
	Diamonds: 6 3	
	Clubs: K J 9 8 4 3	

Spades: J 9 3	N	Spades: 2
Hearts: J 7 4 3		Hearts: Q 10 6
Diamonds: A 2	W E	Diamonds: K Q 10 8 7 4
Clubs: Q 7 6 5	S	Clubs: A 10 2

	Spades: A K Q 8 5 4	
	Hearts: 9 8 5 2	
	Diamonds: J 9 5	
	Clubs: None	

West leads 2D, South plays 6D from dummy, East KD, South 9D.

East considers what to lead next. The Six or Ten of Hearts

63

might be a good idea; still, South might have the Jack and make it later. He decides to continue with Diamonds and leads his Queen. South plays JD. West does a smart thing: he trumps with the JS, knowing that South would trump from dummy anyhow, but cannot overtrump him; and otherwise he has not much chance of making that Jack. South throws away the 3C from dummy.

This is a bad start: three tricks to the defence already. South has to take all the rest to make his contract.

West decides to lead the 5C, hoping that his partner might hold the Ace. South plays JC from dummy. East has the Ace all right, and plays it; but South trumps with the 4S.

Now he's off. He leads the AS; West plays the 3S, 6S from dummy, 2S from East. South continues with the KS; West 9S, dummy 7S, and East throws away 7D.

A count shows that the opposition have no more trumps, so South leads 2H to dummy's Ace, West and East playing small Hearts. Then from dummy South leads KC; East and West play small Clubs and South throws away the 5H.

He leads the 4C from dummy; East plays the 10C, South trumps with 5S, West plays 7C. Now he leads the 8H; West plays 4H, dummy KH, East 10H.

If he can make three more tricks, South is home and dry. He has two trumps left and dummy one, and each of the three must take a trick. South leads the 8C from Dummy, East plays 8D, South trumps with the 8S, and West sees his QC go for a Burton. South leads the 9H and dummy trumps West's JH with the 10S; a 9C lead from dummy, which would win even if South didn't have the QS to trump with.

So South makes his Four Spades Doubled after a start which didn't look promising. But can you see how easily he might have failed if he had not played his cards correctly? As things turned out the King was the only one of North's Clubs which took a trick; it was the skilful use of trumps that made the contract, all six of South's, and one of North's, taking tricks, even though West did manage to make that Jack.

South scores 240 below the line, giving him a game towards the rubber, and 50 above the line for making his doubled contract; no honours, for he held only three of the five top Spades.

Now we will look at something a bit more difficult: the bidding and play of a Grand Slam contract. Here is the deal:

64

Spades: A K Q 8 7 5

Hearts: J 7 4

Diamonds: A 4

Clubs: A 7

Spades: J 10 9 6   N   Spades: 4 3

Hearts: K 6 5   Hearts: Q 9 2

Diamonds: 9   W   E   Diamonds: 6 3 2

Clubs: Q 10 8 4 3   S   Clubs: K 9 6 5 2

Spades: 2

Hearts: A 10 8 3

Diamonds: K Q J 10 8 7 5

Clubs: J

South dealt and bid Two Diamonds. Neither West nor East bid at all, having nothing like the strength for even One Club. North called Two Spades. South showed his other good suit with Three Hearts. North showed control of the other three suits with Three No Trumps. South emphasized his Diamonds with Four Diamonds. North did similarly with Four Spades. South suggested a Slam by bidding Five Diamonds; North showed his Ace of Diamonds with a raise to Six Diamonds, and South, though realizing that Clubs might be the weak spot, took it for granted that North held the Ace on account of his No Trump bid, and went all the way with Seven Diamonds.

West led the 3C, and dummy went down. South realized that Hearts presented a danger; and this Club lead robbed him of what is called a re-entry: that is, a means of getting the lead back into dummy's hand after he had drawn trumps, so that dummy could cash in on the Spades. If the missing Spades happened to be evenly divided between West and East, three each, there should be no problem. (As we can see, they weren't.)

This is how the play went:

West 3C, dummy AC, East 2C, South JC.

Dummy AD, East 2D, South 5D, West 9D.

Dummy 4D, East 3D, South KD, West 4C. Oh dear, thinks South, there's another Diamond out.

South QD, West 5H, dummy 4H, East 6D. Now what to do? Best play out three more Diamond leads, because it will present the opponents with a problem as to what to throw away. So: South JD, West 8C, dummy 5S, East 5C.

At this point both West and East are furiously trying to make up their minds what to discard. West assumes that East holds the KC, as South has played the JC; he doesn't know what Hearts he has, but as the Ace has not gone he wants to keep his King and Six; he wants to keep those four Spades because he could take dummy's fourth Spade lead with his Jack. East sees his KC as a possible winner, and not being sure what Hearts West holds, wants to keep his three to the Queen.

South continues with 10D; West 10C, dummy 7S, East 6C. South 8D, West 6H, dummy 7H, East 3S.

Now South considers whether to keep his last trump in reserve and lead to dummy's Spades. However, he thinks it safest to lead the 7D. Knowing that his partner has the KC to deal with the dummy's 7C, West discards the QC, keeping the KH to protect his partner against a possible finesse. The 8S is played from dummy, and East discards the 4S.

Now South leads the 2S, West plays JS, dummy AS, East 2H.

South leads KS from dummy, East keeps his Hearts and plays 9C, South throws the 3H and West plays 6S.

QS is led from dummy. Now East is the victim of what is known as a 'squeeze'. If he plays the 9H, dummy will lead the JH to South's Ace on the next round; if he lets the KC go, dummy will lead the 7C which is the last Club, then the JH to South's Ace. Here are the two alternative plays of the last three tricks:

    (a) Dummy QS, East 9H, South 8H, West 9S.
        Dummy JH, East QH, South AH, West KH.
        South 10H, West 10S, dummy 7C, East KC.
Or (b) Dummy QS, East KC, South 8H, West 9S.
        Dummy 7C, East 9H, South 10H, West 10S.
        Dummy JH, East QH, South AH, West KH.

I have given this play in detail so that you can understand what a valuable weapon a squeeze is, and how it can come about through skilful play of the cards. It is often particularly useful when playing a No Trump contract.

There was, however, an alternative method of playing the last seven tricks which would equally well gain South his contract against any defence: can you spot it?

If 'we' made that Grand Slam I have just described, we should score 140 below the line – seven tricks bid and made at 20 points each; 1,000 above the line for the Slam; 100 above the line for four honours in South's hand. 140 below the line is more than enough for game, so we draw a line beneath the 140.

Suppose on the second hand we bid Four Hearts in an attempt to snatch a quick rubber, but were doubled and were two down. After the first game we are vulnerable, so our opponents score 500 above the line for the undertricks, 200 for the first and 300 for the second. That's what comes of being greedy and over-confident!

On the third hand our opponents bid and make Four Diamonds, the declarer holding the five honours. They score 80 below the line (4 × 20) and 150 above the line.

On the fourth hand we bid and make Four Spades; 60 (2 × 30) below the line. Now both 'We' and 'They' have a part game in hand.

And on hand five we bid Three No Trumps, and make four. 100 below the line for the three we bid, and 30 above the line for the fourth; and that is two consecutive games, so we get 700 above the line for the rubber. Now the scoring-pad looks like this:

We	They
30	
700	
1,000	150
100	500
140	
	80
60	
100	
2,130	730

67

So subtract 'their' 730 from our 2,130, and we made a gain of 1,400 points on the rubber; not bad at all. Admittedly we had the luck of the deal with that lovely Grand Slam in Diamonds – but if we hadn't played the hand pretty cleverly we could easily have gone down.

There is not much more I have to tell you: if you have taken it all in up to here you are well equipped to start playing good-class Contract Bridge and getting that invaluable experience which will make a good player of you.

Just a word about the etiquette of the game: it matters. Play naturally. If you get a good hand don't show it; if you get a bad one don't look glum. In other words, don't give anything away. Do not try to give your partner any hints about the value of your hand, except what he can gather from your bids.

Never make remarks about the bidding. Don't play a card in an emphatic manner, indicating perhaps that you have more goodies to come. Play smoothly whatever the circumstances. When you are dummy, just lay your cards down neatly and then retire from the game until the next deal.

Stick to the accepted formula for bidding: 'No bid' or 'Pass', 'One Spade', 'Two Hearts', 'Three No Trumps', 'Double', 'Re-double', and so on. Don't be tempted to say things like 'Hmm – I'll chance Four Clubs', or 'Well – I think I'll double'. None of that, please. Keep it plain, simple, and to the point. Keep calm.

SEVEN-CARD RUMMY

Required: 2 packs of cards (with or without Jokers), counters (or matches), pencil and paper

There are no end of variations on the Rummy theme. This is a particularly good one to start with. If you have ever played Mah-jongg, you will realize where Rummy with all its variations came from.

Even within one variant of the game there are optional differences, as you will see. In the interests of harmony it is important to make sure, before you start to play, that all the players are aware of the rules and customs you are adopting.

For real fun, Rummy should be played for small sums of money, but counters can be used; matches can serve as counters.

Any reasonable number, from two upwards, can play. You need two packs of cards, with or without the Jokers, and pencil and paper for scoring. If you use the Jokers, they are 'wild', i.e. you can use a Joker as a substitute for any card. If not, the Twos count as wild cards.

Cut for deal; the player who cuts the highest (or if you so decide, the lowest) card deals; Ace is low. The deal goes round to the left in turn.

Each player contributes a counter to the pool or kitty. Then the dealer deals seven cards to each player, either singly or in three rounds of two and a final one. Cards left over are placed face down in a stack in the middle of the table, the top card being turned face up and placed beside the stack.

The object of the exercise is to collect sets of cards, three or more of the same value, e.g. three Queens, four Eights, and so on; or sequences of cards of the same suit, e.g. Three, Four, Five of Hearts, or Nine, Ten, Jack, Queen of Spades. When all the seven cards in your hand are composed of sets or sequences, or both, you can 'go down'; so you can if six cards are so composed and if the odd card is no higher than a Seven. In this case you declare, for example, 'Down for Five' if your odd card is a Five.

Players will have to decide at the start whether Aces will be regarded as low, i.e. next to Twos in sequences, or high, i.e. next to Kings, or either at the player's option.

So, after the deal, players contemplate for a moment,

deciding what they will try to collect. You have to bear in mind that if another player 'goes down' the cards you are left with will count against you.

First to play is the player to the dealer's left. He can do one of two things: take the exposed card, if he wants it, and discard a card from his hand; or take a chance and pick up the unknown card from the top of the pack, discarding it right away if he doesn't want it or adding it to his hand and discarding another.

The discard is dropped face up on to the discard pile. It is most frustrating to see cards you could have used being covered up.

Play continues round the table in this way until one player 'goes down'. It is usual for him to say 'Rummy' or knock on the table. But you cannot go down immediately you have ex-changed a card: you have to wait until your turn comes round again.

The player who goes down lays his hand face up on the table. The other players do the same. If he has an odd card, having gone down for Five, say, the other players can get rid of any odd Fives they hold by laying them face up on top of his Five. Then the penalty points incurred by the losing players are totted up and recorded. Only the values of cards in their hands which do not form part of a sequence or set count against them. Court cards count 10, Aces 1, other cards their pip-value; wild cards (Jokers or Twos, whichever you are using) count 15.

The player who has gone down takes the 'kitty' and before the next deal each player replenishes it by contributing a counter or coin. The penalty points incurred by the losing players are recorded and a running total kept. When a player's score reaches 100 he is 'bust' and retires from the game, and the game continues until only two players are left to fight it out, winner taking the kitty.

Usually a player who should retire can buy himself back into the game for an agreed sum, starting at the score of the next highest player; but a player can do this only once.

To make it clear: suppose a player goes down with, say, a sequence of Three, Four, Five of Hearts, three Jacks, and an odd Seven of Spades. (Any of these cards may of course be represented by a wild card.) So he says 'Down for Seven' – which is the highest value allowed for his odd card. Another player is left with, say, four Tens, Ace and King of Hearts, and Seven of Hearts. His score is 11: nothing for the set of Tens, nothing for the Seven which he throws on the first player's Seven, 1 for the Ace, and 10 for the King.

Now for some variations which can be agreed beforehand. The player who has made up his hand ready to go down knocks or calls 'Rummy' right away, but play continues round the table until his turn comes again when he lays his hand down. This gives the other players a chance to reduce their penalty points. The kitty can remain intact – replenished on each deal, of course – until the end of the game, when it is divided between the two players left in, in the proportion of 3 to 1, the player with the lowest total score after one had gone down taking the larger share. Lastly: it can be agreed that if a player goes down with a sequence of seven cards, of the same suit of course, this wipes out any score against him.

The deal, of course, goes round the table in the usual way.

There are lots of subtleties in Rummy and you will acquire them in due course. A good Rummy-player, in any variation, must have a good memory. Try to remember which cards have been played, otherwise you may be waiting for a card that never turns up.

Watch carefully the discards of others, especially that fellow sitting on your left. You may very soon realize that he is trying to collect Aces, for example, so you will be able to block his little plan by hanging on to the one you happen to have in your hand – it counts only 1 point against you if you are left with it.

As I said earlier, there are many variations of Rummy. Kuhn Kahn, or Coon Can, is a simpler and perhaps the original form. Kings and Queens and Sequence Rummy, have rather more complicated scoring. Gin Rummy is a two-player, one-pack form with still more complicated scoring and has its own variation called Hollywood. It has been somewhat superseded in the last twenty years by the more elaborate Canasta.

Seven-Card Rummy is a good foundation for becoming expert at any of these variations.

CANASTA

Required: 2 packs of cards (with 2 or 4 jokers), pencil and paper

Canasta reminds me of Mah-jongg as I learned to play it, and is of course a glorified form of Rummy. After the Second World War this game from South America became the rage and was the fashionable card game to play; nowadays we are hearing more and more about further elaborations, which will be explained later.

Canasta can be played two-handed, three-handed, or by four players in two partnerships. You use two packs of cards, including four (sometimes two) Jokers, shuffled together.

The Jokers can be substituted for any card; the Twos are 'wild' also, and as there are eight of them, you have twelve 'wild' cards altogether.

The Threes play an important part in the game. Red Threes have a special function as will be explained. So have black Threes which are 'stop' cards. Red Threes must never be used in melds; black Threes can be used only in melds at the end of the game, and cannot be substituted by wild cards.

Now let's get down to understanding just what it is all about. The idea is to make melds. A meld is made up of three or more cards of a kind, and wild cards can help – with these limitations:

a meld of three cards can contain only one wild card;

a meld of four may contain two wild cards;

a meld of five may contain three wild cards.

A meld of seven cards is called a Canasta (Spanish for 'little basket') and these earn you lots of bonus points. A 'mixed' Canasta, i.e. one with a minimum of four 'natural' cards and three wild cards, is of less value than one of seven natural cards and no wild cards.

If you and I were playing a two-handed game of Canasta it would go something like this. We cut for deal; highest card takes the deal, Ace low.

I win the deal and deal fifteen cards to each of us, singly and alternately. The remainder of the cards becomes the 'stock' which I place face down in the middle of the table. The top card is turned face up and placed beside it. This forms the basis of the 'discard pile', which Americans call the 'pot'. All discarded cards go face up on the pile. For the sake of clarity we will stick to the terms 'stock' and 'pile'.

We pick up our cards and see what fate has in store for us. Place any red Threes you may have in your hand on to the table in front of you right away, and replace them from the stock. These Threes count for or against you at the end of the game.

Arrange your hand with cards of like value, which are possible melds, together, and consider your plan of action.

When you are making melds you must be aware of the values of the cards; very important, this.

Each Joker counts 50;

each Two counts 20;

each Ace counts 20;

each King, Queen, Jack, Ten, Nine, or Eight counts 10;

each Seven, Six, Five, or Four counts 5;

each black Three counts 5.

That isn't the whole of the scoring, but it is all we need at the moment. Now in turn (you first because I dealt), we pick up either the top card of the stock or the top card of the pile, as we wish. Then we discard a card face up on to the pile. It can of course be the one just picked up from the stock.

Suppose, when you look at your hand, you find that you can form a couple of melds. But before you can 'open' you must have a meld worth 50 points, and this, we'll say, you do not have. So you consider the face-up card in the pile, reject it mentally, and take a chance on the top card of the stock. You are lucky; it is an Ace, and as you already have two Aces this gives you a meld worth 60 points with which you could open, putting them down on the table before you discard. Actually it is not wise to put down melds at such an early stage; firstly, it shows me what you are collecting, and secondly, you want to get as many cards in your hand as possible. So how do you do this?

As the game progresses the pile gets bigger, and you can grab it for yourself if you do the right thing. That is, of course, if I don't do it first.

Suppose the top card of the pile happens to be a Queen, and you have in your hand two Queens. Instead of picking up one card, you show your pair and pick up the entire pile and add it to your hand. Until then the pile was 'frozen', and could be taken only with a natural pair. From now on it is unfrozen for you, and you can pick up the whole pile with just one similar card and a wild card; also, you can add the top card to a meld you have laid down and then pick up the rest.

If I want to pick up the pile, I must 'unfreeze' it in the same way. No matter how many cards you pick up in the pile, you discard only one. The cunning bit is for us to stop each other from picking up that pile; so we try to discard cards which we know the opponent doesn't want.

If you find it impossible to block the pile with a discard and I am too clever for you, then there is something else you can do. If you have a black Three in your hand you can put it on the pile, and I cannot in any circumstances take it. I have to take a card from the stock, and the moment I discard and cover up the Three the pile is free again – and the card I have thrown out may be just the one you want.

So black Threes should be saved for use when there is a big discard pile and a risk that your opponent may be able to take it. Remember, too, that a pile containing one or more black Threes is a very useful capture.

So now you see why a black Three is called a 'stop' card. It can be added to a meld only when the player is 'melding out' or ending the game. It must be added to a natural meld (no wild cards) to make three or four; it cannot be made into a mixed canasta. If there is a black Three on top of the pile then you can't use your black Three at all.

Phew – but you will soon remember all these rules. It isn't so bad really.

An even tougher way of freezing the pile is to use a wild card – a Joker if you must, but it is a valuable card to lose – as a stopper. In this case you lay it crosswise on the pile so that the value of the former top card below it can be seen. Then the pile can be taken only with a natural pair matching the top card.

You can see how exciting it all is.

By this time we are both laying melds on the table in front of us and adding to them to make natural or mixed Canastas – a mixed one contains wild cards, remember. You have to sense when to start putting down, because like Rummy, if you are caught with a fistful you will be in real trouble.

Suddenly you meld right out (put down all your cards), we'll suppose, and I am left with four cards in my hand.

Now we come to the scoring, which is an important part of

Canasta. It is best if each player scores separately, or in the four-handed game each side. Being a lazy soul, I always hope that someone else will do all the work.

Consider these bonuses:

Each natural Canasta (no wild cards): 500 points
Each mixed Canasta (one to three wild cards): 300 points
Each red Three: 100 points
All four red Threes: 800 points
Melding out: 100 points
Melding out concealed: 200 points ('Concealed' means that the whole hand is melded out at one turn, including, of course, a Canasta).

So, let's score. You went out with, say:

A Canasta of seven Aces: 500 plus 20 for each Ace	640
A mixed Canasta of four Sixes, two Twos, and a Joker: 300, plus 5 for each Six, plus 20 for each Two, plus 50 for the Joker	410
Four Fours, a Two, and a Joker: 20 plus 20 plus 50	90
Three Sevens	15
Two red Threes, 100 each	200
For melding out	100
So your total is	1,455

My score:	
A mixed Canasta of five Jacks, two Twos: 50 plus 40 plus 300	390
Three Nines and a Joker: 30 plus 50	80
Three Sevens (we were both collecting them)	15
A red Three	100
	585
In my hand (unfortunately) a black Three, two Queens, a Five and a Four: so against me, 5 plus 20 plus 5 plus 5	35
So my total is	550

Had I been caught without any melds the red Threes would have counted 100 against me.

You have done well; I did not do *too* badly.

5,000 is usually the total to be played for. If you should end up with almost the same score above 5,000, the one with the highest score wins.

Some special points to bear in mind:

When your score reaches 1,500 points, you must have 90 points to open; when it reaches 3,000, you must have 120 points to open.

If the first 'up-card', i.e. the face-up card which forms the basis of the pile, happens to be a black Three the dealer must turn up the next card and cover it. The pack is *not* considered frozen.

If the first up-card is a Joker, a wild Two or a red Three, it must be covered and the pack remains frozen until it is taken with a natural pair matching the up-card. Moreover, if the red Three is taken or 'captured' in this way the drawer does not take a card from the stock.

When all cards in the stock have been used up, up-cards from the pile may be picked up as long as they match a meld in your possession. This continues until the up-card cannot be used, and the game is over.

A player left with one card cannot pick up the pile; he must draw from the stock.

Wild cards, Twos and Jokers, can be added to Canastas, but remember that by doing so you would turn a natural Canasta into a mixed one.

Sorry about all this: but it is all part of the game, and very necessary.

Three-handed Canasta is similar to the two-handed game except that each player is dealt thirteen cards, and two canastas are needed to go out. Freezing the pile doesn't help much in this version. Three-handed is a lot of fun.

Four-handed Canasta is a partnership game. It is the best kind of Canasta, played very like the two-handed game but with differences.

As in Bridge, you sit opposite to your partner, with whom you have teamed up by arrangement or have acquired by the usual means of cutting: all cut, those with the highest and lowest cards play together, highest deals.

Use two packs and Jokers as before; players are dealt eleven cards each.

Each player, beginning with the one on the dealer's left, declares and lays down red Threes.

As before, you need 50 points to open, 90 points when the side's score is 1,500 or over, 120 points when it is 3,000 or over. And note this: cards left in a player's hand and not melded count against the partnership, and in scoring their value is subtracted from the total of melds and bonuses – so it is quite possible to start a game with a minus score, in which case either partner can make the first meld without a count of 50.

When one partner has opened correctly his partner is automatically open.

Partners are allowed to add to one another's melds. In fact, it is usual for one partner to keep the score and the other to keep all the melds in front of him. Up-cards can be taken (if the pile is not frozen) and added to melds.

One Canasta is necessary to meld out.

Before the first meld a partner can pick up the pile (if it is not frozen) with a natural pair; after, with one card and a wild card.

A pile can be picked up if a discard matches a card in any meld on the table – belonging to one's own side, of course.

When a game is over the player going out must act as follows: he must draw a card, which can be discarded or used, as the case may be, and then the hand is laid down.

Finally: a player who is ready to meld out, but is not sure whether it will suit his partner, may – though it is not obligatory – ask 'Partner, may I go out?' Those actual words must be used; and the question must be asked before melding or giving any hint that you are about to do so – and only when it is your turn to play. The partner replies 'Yes' or 'No' as the case may be, and the answer is binding. The question can be repeated later.

Canasta is a very good game whether for two, three or four players. Final scores are assessed at one unit per hundred scored – usually anything less than 50 is ignored, and between 50 and 100 regarded as 100 – and if you are playing for money you must decide at the beginning just how much a unit will be worth.

SAMBA
Required: 3 packs of cards with Jokers, pencil and paper

Just as Canasta is an extension of Rummy, Kalooki outdoes Canasta, Samba eclipses Kalooki. For this exciting enlargement of Rummy you need three packs of cards, each pack complete with two Jokers; a total of 162 cards.

Samba is essentially a partnership game. So, as in Bridge, you cut for partners, and the partners sit opposite to each other. You are dealt fifteen cards each.

The three packs have been clumsily shuffled together, and then when the whole heap has been cut the dealer picks up at least enough cards from the top to complete the deal, replacing any surplus back on top.

The deal completed, the balance of the big pack is placed in the middle of the table as usual, the top card then being turned up and placed beside the stock pile in the usual way. Treat this game like Canasta (*see* 72), but with certain differences.

When you draw from stock you pick up two cards instead of one.

When you discard, you discard only one card as in Canasta.

To pick up the pot you must match the face-up card with a real pair in your hand, and they must be shown.

You can pick up the pot if you can put the face card of the pot on to your partner's meld, as long as it is not a completed Canasta.

The pick-ups cannot happen, of course, if stop cards are in place.

Wild cards are Jokers and Twos, and you can stop the pot with wild cards or black Threes.

In forming mixed Canastas only two wild cards may be included.

When you have completed a Canasta you can add cards to it.

When building Canastas you and your partner can build two similar mixed Canastas because there are twelve similar cards of each value as well as wild cards. You won't always manage to complete two at once, but it is worth trying. If you can see in time that the feat will be impossible, you can then just combine the two.

78

The great fun of Samba is to get great fistfuls of cards and to block the pot for everyone else; you have to be bold.

The real difference in Samba is that in this game you can make sequences: you know, Ace, King, Queen, Jack, and so on. A sequence of seven cards is known as a Samba.

To go out you must have two Canastas, and a Samba counts as a Canasta.

Unfinished sequences count as they do in Canasta.

To go down when the score is nil you need 50 points. When the score is 1,500 you must have 90 points; when the score is 3,000 you must have 120 points; when the score is 7,000 you need 150 points. 10,000 is game.

When you go out you get 200 points (Double Canasta). Red Threes are worth 100 points. If you hold all six you get 1,000 points.

A Samba, or sequence of seven of a suit, gets you 1,500. For incomplete Sambas you get 15 for an Ace, 10 for court cards and 5 for others.

Otherwise, the scoring is as Canasta, and so are the penalties.

The great thing is to watch your partner's cards. Help each other; try to get all those cards in the pot and stop your opponents from getting them. Do not be afraid to use wild cards as stoppers.

And finally, Sambas make the points.

FOURSOMES
Required: 1 or 2 packs of cards

Any number can play. As each player should receive not less than six cards, you may need two packs. Remove the Jokers.

Cut for deal; lowest card cut indicates the dealer.

Cards are dealt one at a time to each player in turn; if at the end there are not enough cards left to complete a round, the remaining cards are put to one side without any player seeing their faces.

Players pick up their hands and see what they have got. The idea of the game is to collect foursomes, i.e. sets of four cards of the same value, four Kings, four Tens, four Sixes, and so on.

The player to the left of the dealer begins. Let's say that he holds the Queens of Clubs, Diamonds and Spades. He looks around at the other players, picks on someone and says 'May I have the Queen of Hearts, please?'

If he is lucky the other player hands it over. The first player now has the foursome of Queens and puts them face down on the table in front of him. Then he has another turn; note that you must have at least one of a foursome or you can't ask for another.

This time, perhaps, he has two Tens and asks another player for either of the missing ones. He is unlucky: the player hasn't got it, and the turn passes to him. He says 'Sorry, no; but so-and-so, may I have the Ace of Diamonds?' or whatever he wants.

Yes, you'll realize by now that this is the old game of Happy Families played with ordinary cards. If you have never played Happy Families and don't know what I'm talking about, it doesn't matter.

So the battle continues, and the real fun begins when players begin to remember who has asked for what; a player who has asked, unsuccessfully, for a Jack, for example, must hold at least one and probably more. So when the turn passes to a player who has a Jack he will remember this, and relieve the unlucky one of perhaps three that he has been trying to make into a foursome.

When a player receives the card he needed to complete his last foursome, and has no odd cards left – but not before – he can start asking for complete foursomes: 'So-and-so, may I have the Aces, please?' And as before he can go on amassing complete foursomes until he has the lot, or until he asks wrongly. Then the turn passes to the player who says 'No'. This makes for lots of fun at the end of a game, sometimes: you may have two players with one foursome each and another who has all the rest; in his eagerness he makes a mistake and asks the wrong player. That gives him the opportunity to clean up!

The game ends when one player has the lot. The moment you have lost all your cards you are out of it until the next game.

This game is sometimes called 'Authors'; I can't think why. Some people play it regardless of the suits, simply asking, for example, for a Queen or a Ten or whatever. It isn't half as much fun.

Foursomes is a very pleasant, easy-to-learn family game.

FARMERS
Required: 1 pack of cards, counters (or matches)

The more players the merrier. You need a pack of cards with the Eights and Sixes removed, except the Six of Hearts which is left in: total forty-five cards.

Court cards count 10, pip cards their face value, Ace counting 1.

Cut to decide which player will be banker; lowest card takes the bank.

The banker shuffles the cards and places them face down in front of the player on his left.

This player picks up one card. Let us suppose that it is a court card, value 10. The game is to hold two cards, and two only, which have a combined value of 16.

He picks up a second card, hoping for the Six of Hearts, but it is an Ace, total 11. This is not good enough, so he picks a third card from the top of the pack. Suppose this is a Five; he discards the Ace, making his total now 15. If the player wishes he can try again and keep on trying.

If he tries again and picks up a Nine, he can then keep this one and discard the court card; total now 14. This picking up and throwing away can continue as long as the player's total does not exceed 16.

If the total of 16 is exceeded you must be honest and stop. The other players do not know whether you have stopped because you are satisfied, or because you had to.

The player now shuffles all discarded cards back into the pack and puts it in front of the next player, and so on.

When the cards reach the banker, he does not pick cards but orders that all hands be turned face up on the table so that the pay-out can begin.

Players with exactly 16 get as many counters as there are players from the banker.

Any player holding 16 including the Six of Hearts is paid two counters by each other player, including the banker.

Players holding more than 16 pay one counter to the banker for every pip above 16. Players holding less than 16 pay the banker a flat rate of one counter.

Quite good fun, this. All you have to do is to buy a farm and engage enough staff.

DOMINO

Required: 1 pack of cards (no Jokers), a table with plenty of space

For centuries we have heard the clatter of dominoes in clubs and pubs. I can't even begin to guess how many of you play dominoes; here is something very like it, but unlike the noisy game you know this one is as silent as the Secret Service. It is a game for two or more players.

Shuffle the pack, and deal cards one at a time to the players in turn until there are none left. If there are three or five or six players that will mean that some have a card more than others; don't worry, the deal passes round the table in the usual way so things even themselves out.

The player on the dealer's left is the first to play, and the turn passes round clockwise. You need a Seven to open. If you have a Seven, you put it face up in the middle of the table. If you haven't you 'knock' or pass. The first player with a Seven opens the game.

Suppose it is the Seven of Diamonds: the next player can do one of three things. He can place a Six of Diamonds on one side of the Seven; or an Eight of Diamonds on the other side of the Seven; or a Seven of a different suit above or below the Seven of Diamonds. If he cannot play any of these he must knock.

Each player plays only one card when it is his turn, unless he knocks.

So you build left and right of the Sevens in sequence, in the same suit, or above and below with Sevens of different suits. Automatically all the suits line up and at the finish you would find the four suits in four rows one above the other. The player to go out (i.e. to have played all his cards) is the winner. You can play for new pence if it makes you happy.

Strategy is the same as in the mother game. If, say, you played that Seven of Diamonds and also hold the Six and Eight and no other Diamonds, you should try to hang on to them as long as you can and so hold up other players and force them to pass. In other words, by holding cards that you can play later, but at the same time being lucky enough to have alternative cards to play, you increase your chance of winning.

As with Dominoes proper, there is a lot of luck in the draw, and, however crafty you may be, good cards do help.

A good game, this: no problems, no worry, no fuss – and it's very hush-hush!

HOODLUM
Required: 1 or 2 packs of cards, counters (or matches)

A game for three or more players: but if there are more than four players you will have to dip into a second pack, because each player starts off with a complete suit, one all the thirteen Spades, another all the Hearts, and so on.

About fifty years ago this was hailed as a completely new game. Physically it is simple to play, but mentally it is a question of bluff and counter-bluff like Poker. The game need not be taken too seriously; it can be played for fun or reward. You know – for money, counters, matches, or whatever.

As our American friends credit the English as saying, 'Jolly good game, this.'

So each player is ready with his complete suit. As there appear to be no rules about it, let us say that the player on the left of the dealer plays first and play follows clockwise round the table as usual – except that he is not strictly speaking a 'dealer', he's the one who dishes out the suits.

Before play begins the dealer explains that in the first round the highest card will win, in the next round the lowest card, and so on alternately, through the thirteen rounds. It will be as well if he becomes the caller and before each round says 'Highest' or 'Lowest' as the case may be. Ace, by the way, counts high. So the players put their cards face down in front of them in turn. Subsequent cards go face down on top of them so that each player finishes up with a neat pile of thirteen cards.

Now, you will realize that a great deal of thought has to be exercised. Do you try to take the first trick, or not? The score sheet on the next page shows why you should be careful. As you play, round by round, the scores get higher. So do you try to play the highest or lowest cards, as the case may be, on the earlier rounds, or hold back your high or low cards with the idea of winning the later, more rewarding rounds?

You must bear in mind that the other players have similar thoughts. Perhaps a Seven will win the first round; perhaps a Six will win the second. You may be sure that highest and lowest cards are being saved for later use. In fact, the more you think about this game, the more you realize how much there is to think about!

So round by round it goes, Highest, Lowest, Highest, Lowest, for the thirteen rounds. At the end all the players turn their piles of cards face up in front of them, and with pencil and paper the scores are recorded:

Round		Winner scores	Next best scores
1	Highest	3	1
2	Lowest	4	2
3	Highest	5	2
4	Lowest	6	3
5	Highest	7	3
6	Lowest	8	4
7	Highest	9	4
8	Lowest	10	5
9	Highest	11	5
10	Lowest	12	6
11	Highest	13	6
12	Lowest	14	7
13	Highest	15	7

But: when on any round two players tie for the highest card, or lowest card, they score only 2 points each; the same applies if more than two tie. And if two or more players are equally next best, they score nothing. As you look through this scoring table you will realize that it is very easy to memorize. In any case, you can have the book open at this page for reference.

So with all the players having their piles of cards face up, the scorer looks at the face card, which was of course that played to the first round, and jots down the scores. Then each player turns over the first card to disclose the next, and so the scoring goes. When all the thirteen rounds have been scored you settle up, according to what you are playing for, and pick up your cards and play the next game.

Do try this. It really is a jolly good game.

PIP-PIP

Required: 2 packs of cards without Jokers (well shuffled together), plenty of table space, pencil and paper

A good game for from three to eight players. The object of the game is to take tricks containing Twos, Aces, Kings, Queens, and Jacks (note that in this game the Two ranks higher than the Ace). Each Two, in the tricks you have taken by the end of the game, counts 11 points; each Ace, 10; each King, 5; each Queen, 4; each Jack, 3.

Before the deal the double pack is cut for trumps. As in other games with trumps, a trump however small beats a card of any other suit. But as you will see, the trump suit keeps changing during the game.

The dealer deals seven cards to each player, and the rest of the pack, or stock, is placed face down in the middle of the table. The player on the dealer's left leads, and play goes clockwise round the table as usual, the winner of each trick leading to the next one.

Players must follow suit if possible, otherwise trump or discard a card of another suit. If two players play identical cards – say, for example, a player leads the King of Spades and the only Spade you hold is the other King, so you have to play it – the second, not the first, of the two is regarded as the winner. So you would take his King of Spades with yours.

After playing a card to a trick, each player replaces it by taking the top card of the stock. This continues until there are fewer cards left in the stock than there are players; the remaining cards in the stock are turned face up and left there, and the remaining tricks are played out.

The feature which gives the game its name is this: whenever a player holds the King and Queen of the same suit, not the trump suit, he calls 'Pip-pip' and lays them face up in front of him. For this he scores 50 points, and the trump suit is changed to that of the King and Queen. You can call 'Pip-pip' as soon as you have drawn a card, if you like; you can call right at the start of the game, even before a card has been played, if you happen to be dealt the King and Queen of a suit different from the trump suit. You are not obliged to call if you think it would be an advantage not to, or to wait, but you run the risk of losing the 50-point bonus.

After you have 'pip-pipped' you can play the King or Queen when you like; you can 'pip-pip' twice in the same suit but not of course with the same King or Queen.

More than one player can call 'Pip-pip' during the play of the same trick; each scores the 50 points and the trump suit changes to that of the player who called last.

It is best for one player to act as scorer, with pencil and paper, noting the 50-point bonuses as they are scored; then at the end of the game each player turns over his tricks and counts up his Twos, Aces, Kings, Queens, and Jacks, for scoring.

When I was a schoolboy we used to call out 'Pip-pip Maria' and the reply was 'Pip-pip Maria yourself, my name's Violet!'

I PROMISE

Required: 1 pack of 52 cards without jokers, pencil and paper

This is a good game for from three to seven players. It is also known as 'Oh Well!' and 'Oh Hell!' but I think that 'I Promise' is a better name.

The dealer, chosen by the usual ritual of cutting for the lowest card, deals out the whole pack one card at a time, making sure that all players have the same number of cards. This only happens exactly and automatically when there are four players, of course; so he stops when he has dealt the last card to himself and hasn't enough left for another round. The one, two, three, or four cards remaining, when there are three, five, six, or seven players are put to one side, unseen. Does that sound complicated? It isn't really. Note that these unused cards should be returned to the pack before it is shuffled for the next deal, otherwise clever players may deduce what they are, which rather spoils the game.

So you all pick up your cards, study them, and consider how many tricks you can safely promise to make. The player on the dealer's left begins, saying for example 'I promise to make three'. The next player makes his promise which might be 'None', and so on all the way round.

Just to make sure that there is no argument later, a player designated as scorer, with pencil and paper, writes down all the promises: Bill 3, Mary 0, John 6, and so on.

Before play starts, the dealer turns up the last card dealt to himself to denote the trump suit. As usual, a trump card however small beats a card of any other suit however high.

So the game begins. The player on the dealer's left leads the first card and the other players follow suit, or if they cannot follow suit they either trump, or discard something not wanted. The player who takes the trick leads for the next. In fact, this is Whist all over again – but with one big difference.

You have, shall we say, promised to make four tricks. Oh yes you did: that was what you meant when you said 'I promise to make four'. So you must try to make good your promise, precisely. You must try to take four tricks, or whatever it was, no more, and no less. And to keep your promise is very difficult indeed, and that is what makes this a really good and fairly skilful game.

When the game is over, the reckoning begins. For making your promise exactly you score 10 points, plus one point for each trick. So if for example you promised four, your score is 10 plus 4, total 14.

But if you make more, or less tricks than your promise you score 1 point for each trick with no bonus.

A running total is kept and the first player to reach 100 is the winner. This is a good game to play with a kitty, each player chipping in with the same amount at the start, and the winner taking all.

A promise of 'None' is not easy to achieve, though the more players there are the more chance there is: the other players gang up on you to force you to take a trick. Similarly, when you have made your promised tricks the others unite to try to compel you to take another and lose your bonus!

A very, very good game – I promise!

CHEAT

Required: 1 pack of 52 cards (if there are more than four players, it is best to use 2 packs shuffled together)

A game for the family in which one is taught to lie unscrupulously. Oh dear! However, it's all fun and games.

Having shuffled them, deal round the table in the usual way until all the cards have been dealt.

The game itself is simple. The player to the left of the dealer begins, playing one card face down onto the table. He can try playing two together, but if he is challenged he is in trouble.

So the first player puts a card face down and names its value, for example saying 'Eight'. The next player puts a card on top of it and says 'Nine'. This is where the cheating comes in. The cards have to follow, or be alleged to follow, in sequence, up to the King and then starting with the Ace again. So, you see, you have to cheat sometimes, however much you want to be honest.

All the players are watching one another's faces and reactions. Any time a player thinks that another is cheating, he challenges him. If he is in fact cheating he has to pick up all the cards on the table and add them to his hand. If however he was telling the truth, the challenger has to take the cards. So be careful when you cheat, and even more careful when you accuse someone else of cheating.

If you are cunning, you can calculate what value of card you will have to play on the next and subsequent rounds, that's supposing the play goes round without a challenge, and so make sure to keep cards you will need and not discard them when cheating.

After a challenge, the player who has picked up the cards plays a card to start the next round. The winner is the player who gets rid of all his cards first, which I suppose makes him the biggest cheat of all.

There is not much playing skill about this game, but among friends and in a family where the players are well known to one another it becomes a real battle of wits.

Shh! – did I make it clear that you can try to get rid of extra cards by holding two or more so that they look like one? Just don't be caught doing it, that's all. You will have to pick up the lot: and serve you jolly well right.

DRY GAME
Required: 1 pack of cards, pencil and paper

At least, that's what the original title means when it's translated into English. You see, at a party I met a distinguished architect who said that he was Greek and that his name was Giorgalakis. I asked him about card games and he was kind enough to tell me about two very simple ones, the first being the Dry Game.

Two, three, or four players: you need a pack of 52 cards without Jokers. Cut for deal, the highest card cut taking the deal, Ace high.

A game is over when there are insufficient cards left in the pack for another deal – three deals with two players, two deals with three players, one deal with four players. Personally, I don't see why up to eight players should not take part – or even more if you use two packs shuffled together.

The dealer gives each player six cards, dealing three at a time, then deals the next four cards into a face-up pile in the middle of the table. The undealt cards are put to one side for the next deal.

The player on the dealer's left plays first, placing a card face up on to the pile. If his card is the same value as the top (face) card of the pile, he takes the lot, putting the cards he takes face down in front of him. In this case the next player plays a face-up card to start a fresh pile. Otherwise, the second player plays a card on to the pile, taking the pile if it matches or leaving it there if it doesn't. So the game progresses.

Should the pile consist of only one card and the player whose turn it is can match it, this is called a 'dry' trick and he receives an immediate 10 points.

Jacks are fortunate cards to hold because a Jack can take the pile whatever the value of the top card. So you save your Jacks, if you can, to take a single-card dry trick, or a big pile, especially when it contains scoring cards (see p 93).

Whenever the pile has been taken the player due to play puts down a card to start a new pile. And when the players have played their six cards the dealer deals fresh hands of six cards, and another four cards on top of the pile.

When the game is over, that is, when there are not enough cards for a fresh deal, the players turn up the cards they have taken and score as follows:

Two of Diamonds counts	2
Ten of Diamonds counts	2
Every Jack counts	1
Player who has most cards scores	3
Player who has most Clubs scores	3
And as I have said, every dry trick counts	10

I asked Mr Giorgalakis why the Clubs scored, and he said he didn't know, but he was sure that the Greeks had a word for it.

LADIES' GAME
Required: 1 pack of cards, pencil and paper

This title too is literally translated from the Greek; it is the second game explained to me by Mr Giorgalakis. He said that it was called Ladies' Game because it is so simple that anyone can understand it, even the ladies.

Two or more players: a pack of 52 cards.

Cut for deal, the highest card denoting the dealer for the first game. By the way, in this and the Dry Game, as in most card games, the deal passes clockwise round the table to the first dealer's left.

The dealer deals six cards to each player, then the next four cards face up on to the table but not on top of one another: all four cards are exposed.

The first player, the one to the dealer's left, can take from the table any card which he can match with one from his hand: a King takes a King, a Four takes a Four, and so on. Or he can take two or more cards whose value adds up to a card he plays from his hand: for example, with a Nine he could take a Four and a Five, or three Threes, or a Six and a Two and an Ace; with a King (court cards count ten) he could take two, or three, or four cards the value of which added up to ten. (Well, that's a long and unwieldy sentence to be sure.)

If a player can't take anything, or if there is nothing left on the table to take, he just has to discard a card to the middle of the table by the side of any cards already there.

This goes on until all the players have played their six cards; then if there are enough cards left in the pack (according to the number of players) the dealer deals again, six cards each and four in the middle of the table.

At the end of the game the players turn up the cards they have taken, which they have kept in a face-down pile in front of them, and score exactly as for Dry Game which was described just before this one – so turn back a page, please.

It may, of course, happen that at the end of a game there are cards left in the middle of the table which no player has been able to take, and there are insufficient cards left in the pack for a fresh deal: never mind, reckon your scores, gather all the cards together, shuffle the pack and start a fresh game.

Gambling games

DRAW POKER
Required: 1 pack of cards, 'chips' (counters or matches)

The great, the romantic game of Poker conjures up visions of the Klondike and the Wild West.

I well remember when that great pianist, Solomon, was in India to entertain the troops and was placed in my care, he asked me if I could play Poker. I said that I could, a little. This was my undoing. Every night after his concerts we played well into the small hours, and he relieved me of all my spare cash. He was a wonderful pianist too.

It is simple enough to acquire the basic principles of Poker, but the playing of the game itself is another matter – quite, quite another matter. This is a game which is played without a wink or a smile. A game played with skill, cunning, subtlety; with a knowledge of human character, and with courage.

Poker has endless ramifications; something like a hundred 'laws', and points of 'etiquette' as well – and even these are not universally accepted, but vary from place to place. There are different ways of betting, and variations within the game itself. I sometimes think that every 'school', or group of regular players, must have its own individual idiosyncracies.

No one person could be familiar with the lot; and it would have to be a very big book which set out to explain and define everything to do with Poker. So the best thing I can do is to give you the basic idea and some easy variations, which will be plenty for family play. If later on you join in a game with experienced players they will gladly tell you just how they play, and knowing the basic idea, at least you won't look like a complete novice.

Poker is played for money stakes, however small. Played for fun, it's fun, but not quite the real thing. With nothing to lose, a player can afford to be reckless and illogical, and spoil the game.

It is usual to use 'chips' to represent money – cash would be inconvenient. Chips are counters, generally of different colours representing different values: white for 1, red for 5, blue for 10, perhaps. You can use matches if you have plenty available. For simplicity we'll use the term 'chip' to mean one unit. One person generally sells the chips and buys them back after the session.

Poker is a game of cool calculation and bluff. Your opponents should never be quite sure whether you are bluffing or not, and you are in the same position about them. If you can convince an opponent that your hand is better than his you may break his nerve; he throws in, and you collect without even showing what you hold.

But it would be silly to bluff all the time. Opponents would soon tumble to your game and 'call your bluff' – and you would be the loser.

Enough of all this. Let's try to explain the game.

You need a pack of cards, without Jokers for this particular variety; chips or matches or something; two or more players; and lots of luck.

Someone deals cards round until one player gets a Jack; then he is the first dealer. In subsequent games the deal moves clockwise round the table.

The pack is shuffled by the dealer and cut (if he wishes) by the player on his right. Some players do not shuffle again during the session; they just assemble the pack and cut. But it is more usual to 'burn' the bottom card of the pack after cutting, i.e. to show it to everyone and then turn it face up. So when you have gone through the pack once you see the face-up card, and shuffle and cut again.

Cards are dealt clockwise one at a time until each player has five. The remainder of the pack is placed face down in front of the dealer. You pick up your cards and look at them. What you are looking for is one of the following combinations, in descending order of value:

Royal straight flush. That is Ace, King, Queen, Jack and Ten, all of the same suit. It beats everything.

Straight flush. The same, but not headed by an Ace: for example, 10, 9, 8, 7, 6 of one suit. If two players have straight flushes, the highest wins. In this combination the Ace counts as One; so the lowest straight flush is 5, 4, 3, 2, Ace.

Fours. Four cards of the same value, e.g. four Tens. Highest wins.

Full house. Three cards of the same value, and two of another value. For example, three Kings and two Twos. This would be beaten by three Aces and two Twos – or two Kings and three Twos would be beaten by two Kings and three Threes. Get the idea?

Flush. Any five cards of the same suit, not in sequence. One flush beats another with its highest card; or if the highest cards are of the same value, then the next highest are compared, and so on.

Straight. Five cards in sequence regardless of suits, the Ace ranking either high (above King) or low (below Two). Between two straights, the one with the highest card wins, as with a straight flush.

Threes. Three cards of the same value and two odd cards. Highest wins.

Two pairs. Two pairs (cards of the same value) and an odd card. Hand with the highest pair wins. If highest pairs are the same value, the hand with the next highest pair wins. If both pairs are the same value, the hand with the highest odd card wins.

One pair. One pair of cards of the same value, and three odd cards. As before, the hand with the highest pair wins; if two hands have pairs of equal value, that with the highest odd card wins; if these are the same, that with the next highest odd card, and so on.

Finally; if two players have none of the above and have been bluffing each other, the hand with the highest card wins – or the next highest, and so on. Such hands are called Ace high, King high, or whatever is the highest card.

If it happens – which is hardly ever – that even after applying all these yardsticks there is still a tie between two hands, then the players concerned divide the stakes.

So there you are. You would like to pick up a royal straight flush, but it doesn't happen once in half a million deals. So almost always you have to settle for something much lower. But you maintain a 'poker face' and show neither triumph nor despair, and have an air of confidence at least as long as you stay in the betting.

If you always bet as though you hold a royal straight flush, you'll soon be broke! That's bluffing carried to excess.

Suppose we just consider your hand. You have picked up two Sixes, a Three, a Nine, and an Ace. What to do?

You have a pair, so keep them. Usually, though not necessarily, you discard the other three cards. When your turn comes the dealer will ask you how many cards you want; you say 'Three' and discard three, and he gives you three from the top of the pack.

They might be three Kings, giving you a full house. Better still, two more Sixes and an odd card, giving you fours. Or three that are no use to you at all.

Alternatively, you could throw away two cards and keep the two Sixes and the Ace. Who knows, luck might give you two Aces, or a Six and an Ace, or two Sixes. Or nothing. This is the gamble.

Again, if you are an experienced player pitted against some timid ones and you hold a fairly high pair you might decide to throw away no cards at all. This might put the wind up the other players, who are led to believe that you have such a good hand that it can't be improved by the draw.

I am not advising you to do this: you have to feel your way towards that kind of bluff. I am just trying to show you how many ways you can think.

If you throw away four cards and keep only one, or if you throw away all five and draw a fresh hand altogether, you are fairly telling the others that you have nothing; only a terrific stroke of luck could give you a good hand now – though mind you, if you are playing with an unshuffled pack anything can happen.

Now, remember that although we are dealing only with your hand, all the other players are busy plotting and scheming as well.

You have decided to throw away three cards. Discards go into the middle of the table, face down. The dealer, when your turn (clockwise) comes, gives you three cards from the pack. They are rewarding: you pick up an Ace, a Three, and another Six. So you threw away an Ace but picked one up. More important, you now have three Sixes, which gives you quite a good hand: so you sit tight. All the other players are dealt with, and you watch the draw carefully: watch faces, watch how many cards are thrown out and picked up, watch everything.

Now for the betting. As I have said, there are different ways of betting, but for family play here is as good a way as any.

Before the deal you all put one chip (we'll use the term whether or not you are using chips) into the kitty or pot. That's just to play. If when you pick up your hand you feel that even by drawing more cards you haven't much of a chance, you throw in and sit the game out; and will then forfeit your chip.

Even if you have discarded and drawn, you may still decide

that your hand is not worth betting on, so you drop out and, again, lose your chip. But that is all you have lost. Really careful players throw in most of the time, especially if stakes are high; it can become a bore. If all the players throw in, the chips stay in the kitty for the next game.

So now you are ready to bet. You have put in one chip to play and you are holding three Sixes. At the beginning of the session a limit for betting and raising was decided on: let's suppose that two chips is the limit.

So you push two chips forward and say 'I bet two' or just 'Two'. The player on your left considers this and feels that his hand is better than yours – or so he wants you to think – so he raises you two: that is, he puts down two chips to cover your bet and another two for the 'raise'. Let's say the next player drops out, and the next, and the next.

Back to you. If you suspect that your only remaining opponent is bluffing, you can put in two more chips to cover his raise and another two to raise him again.

Or, you can put in two to cover his raise and say 'I'll see you'. Then you both show your hands and the highest hand takes the lot, bets and kitty. When you see his hand you get an idea of the way he bets.

When there are more than two players fighting it out and you do not wish to 'see', just put in an amount equal to the raise and say 'I'll stay'. You are still in the game and await events.

Suppose that you keep on raising and your opponent loses his nerve and throws in; you just collect without showing your cards, so he will never know just what you held.

Well: that's a rough idea, and with no more information than this you could have a game of Poker right away without coming to too much harm. Family Poker, anyhow.

You have, of course, been playing Draw Poker. Regular players indulge in all kinds of variations of the game. At times a different variation is played each round. Usually it is up to the dealer to call the tune.

I played Poker with Americans during the war, in Persia, and they seemed to have endless variations which they felt broke the monotony. Here are a couple which are fairly popular and not too way-out.

JACKPOTS. And Queenpots, Kingpots, and Acepots.

Before he deals the dealer can call Jackpots. This just means that you must have two Jacks, or better, in your hand before you can 'open', i.e. make your first bet. All players 'chip in' before the deal, usually one chip. This is not a bet, of course; it's called the 'ante'. Sometimes only the dealer antes, with one or two chips.

If you are sitting on the dealer's left and it is your turn: you can open if you have two Jacks or any better hand. But it could happen that you wanted to discard one of them: suppose for example that you held Jack of Hearts and Jack, Eight, Four, and Two of Spades. You would discard the Jack of Hearts in the hope of picking up another Spade for a Flush. But don't throw it in with the other discards; keep it near to you, so that if challenged later you can show that you did in fact have two Jacks.

If you do not want to open because you prefer to wait and see how the land lies, you can pass, or 'check' as the Americans say. Hence the phrase 'bet or check'. If someone else opens you can enter the game: call, raise, or drop out.

If no player opens, hands are thrown in, everyone 'sweetens' the pot with another chip, and there is a fresh deal. Usually, it's Queenpots this time; and some players double the limit. If all pass again, the next deal is Kingpots; then Acepots; then Two Pairs to open. Then it would revert to Acepots and so on down to Jackpots again. But if any one of the pots is opened, it's back to Jackpots. In this variation the pot can be really worth having.

DEUCES WILD. Draw Poker with all deuces, or Twos, 'wild' – that is, capable of being substituted for any desired card – can become very wild indeed. Some players regard five of a kind, e.g. four Aces and a wild card – five Aces – as ranking as the highest hand, beating a royal straight flush. Others stipulate that a wild card must represent some specified card not held by the player, in which case there can be no such thing as fives. But note that 'naturals' beat wild cards: for example, an Ace and two wild cards can represent three Aces, and would beat three Kings; but would lose to three genuine Aces, or two Aces and one wild card.

This game can be made wilder still by adding one or two Jokers, or by making Threes wild as well; but for me, deuces wild is quite enough.

Some players play 'One-eyed Jacks wild', which means the

Jacks of Hearts and Spades, which are in profile on the cards. Some play 'All One-Eyes', meaning the one-eyed King of Diamonds as well. Some use a Joker but call it 'The Bug'; it can stand for an Ace or for any card in filling a flush or a straight. These variations can be amusing – or they can get rather silly.

That's enough about wild cards for the time being, anyhow.

STUD POKER. Experienced players often favour this Poker game; its variations are very popular and may appeal to you.

There is no 'ante'. The dealer deals one card face down to each player in turn. This is called the 'hole card'. A second card each is dealt face up; then the dealing stops for the moment for a round of betting.

The players take a 'peek' at their hole cards and along with their exposed cards can size up the situation. The player with the highest exposed card is the first to bet – or if two exposed cards are equal in value, the 'elder' player of the two, i.e. the one to whom the cards were dealt first.

If he bets, those who follow can either 'stay' by covering the bet, or raise by covering it and adding another equal stake, or drop out, in which case turning over the face-up card.

When the dealer has had his turn, he deals a third card face up to those players still in the game. The same procedure is followed. Then a fourth card face up; then a fifth. More bets are made each time.

It is most important, in fairness to the other players, not to 'drop' out of turn; nor to let anyone see the faces of your cards after you have dropped out.

The unknown value of the hidden hole cards makes this game very exciting, and wonderful for bluffing. The limit should be kept fairly low or losses and winnings can mount up. Incidentally, as many as ten players can take part with only one pack in use.

These variations on the Poker theme should satisfy you for the time being.

PONTOON
Required: 1 or 2 packs of cards

Also known as *Vingt-et-un*, Twenty-one, and Black Jack, this easy-to-learn gambling game must have been played the world over. The gambling element is inseparable from the game; play for counters or matches if you must, but with nothing to lose players get reckless and ruin the game. With even the smallest stakes, it becomes interesting.

You need a pack of cards without Jokers; any number of players, but if more than, say, seven play use two packs shuffled together.

The idea of the game is to get a total of 21, or as near as possible to 21 without exceeding it, with two or more cards. Aces count either one or eleven at the player's option, court cards count ten, other cards their face value.

A total of 21 with two cards, which of course has to be an Ace and a court card, or an Ace and a Ten, is called 'Pontoon' and beats any other combination – and, as you will see, wins the 'bank'.

If the game is new to you, perhaps what I have said so far won't convey much, so let's assume that we are playing a game, just three of us. As the betting is so integral a part of Pontoon, I will assume that we are adopting the simplest system: I'll explain the more complicated possibilities, which make it more of a gamble, later.

First of all, someone has to be the banker. We draw cards from the pack and the one who draws the highest, Ace high, takes the bank to start with and does the dealing. Say I get the bank. I keep it until one of you two gets a Pontoon then, as long as I haven't a Pontoon too, he takes over the bank on the next round.

We have agreed on our stakes, say three pennies as the maximum bet.

I shuffle the pack, let the player on my right cut it, and I complete the cut. Then starting with the player on my left I deal one card face down to each player including myself.

We peep at our cards and put a stake on the table in front of us – that is, you and the other chap do; I don't because I'm the banker.

Suppose the first player has been dealt a Six. That's not very

103

promising: he stakes a minimum bet, one penny. You have a Ten: that's better. Your second card might be an Ace; or it might well be another ten or a court card – remember, there are 16 cards in the pack with a value of ten. So you stake two pence.

I deal each of you a second card, having seen your stakes, and one to myself.

The first player gets a Nine, making his total 15. That's too low to 'stick' with, in fact most players regard it as unethical to rest content at less than 16; on the other hand, it's a bit too near to 21 to risk 'buying' another card. So he says 'Twist me one'; that means a free card, which he does not have to buy, and I deal it to him face up. It turns out to be a Seven, making his total 22 – over 21 so he is 'bust' and out of the game, losing his stake.

Now I turn to you. Your second card is a Nine. Total 19; not too bad, though an Ace or Ten would have been better. It would be silly to buy or twist another card, so you say 'Stick'.

Now I turn over my cards: an Ace and a Nine, total 10 or 20. Even if I choose to regard it as 10, its obviously not worth risking another card: so I say 'Pay 21'. I have only you to beat; I have already drawn the first chap's penny. You turn over your cards; only 19, so I take your two pence. I collect the cards and put them under the rest of the pack – you only shuffle when the bank changes hands – and deal around again.

The first player gets a Two. A low card like this holds out a possibility of a hand which beats anything except a pontoon: five cards totalling less than 21, or exactly 21, usually called a five-card trick. So he stakes two pence.

You get an Ace. As the chances are so good of getting a Ten or a court card for your second card, making a pontoon, you stake the maximum, three pence.

After all players have received their second cards, the banker finishes with each before he goes on to the next. I deal a second card to each of us. The first player gets a Three. Very promising: he can't increase his original stake on any one additional card, but he can buy his third card for another two pence. It's another Two: that's a total of seven with three cards. He buys a fourth card for another two pence. An Eight this time; total 15, and getting perilously near to 21. He doesn't risk buying the fifth card, so he says 'Twist me one'; it's a Five, so he's all right.

He's sorry he didn't buy it.

If, by the way, his fourth card had been a Four, making his total 11, it would have been impossible for him to 'bust', so it would not have been fair to buy his fifth card; he would have laid the four down face up and 'twisted' one.

Back to you, with an Ace for your first card. If your second had been the ten or court card you hoped for, making a pontoon, you would have showed it by turning over the Ace face up and laying the cards down. But it's another Ace. You have the option of 'splitting' two Aces, and playing them separately, which you do, staking another three pence on the second. We regard them just as if your hands were two separate players.

So I deal you a second card on each. The first is a King; you turn up the Ace indicating a pontoon. Good for you; I can't beat you unless I too have a pontoon. (One thing: on split Aces you don't take the bank).

The second card on your other Ace is a Seven. Eight or eighteen; you might as well play for safety and stick.

Now I turn up my cards: a Four and a Five. I shall in any case have to pay out on your pontoon, so I may as well try for a five-card trick, which by the way is also called 'five and under'. I turn up my third card; a Two, total 11. Good so far. I turn up my fourth; a Six, total 17. I could stick at this and pay 18 and over; but I already know that I should have to pay the first player, and you on your pontoon if not your other lot, so I may as well risk another card and hope that it's no higher than a Four, in which case I should have only your pontoon to pay.

I'm unlucky: my fifth card is a Jack and I'm well and truly bust. So I pay the first player his total stake, six pence, and you three pence for your 18 and another three pence for your pontoon. But as you got it with split Aces, I don't hand over the bank to you.

So the game goes: I continue as banker until one of you gets a pontoon, when you take over the bank, shuffle the pack, and carry on.

Just to summarize this basic betting system: players agree on a maximum stake, which should be at least three units to give a bit of flexibility, allowing you to stake, one, two, or three according to the potentialities of your first card. If you want more cards after you have seen your second you can buy them, for an amount not exceeding your original stake; or twist them for free, in which case you get them face up so the banker can see them. If you split Aces you can place your original stake on each. But having once twisted a card you can't buy, you must carry on twisting: this applies to the five-card trick. You declare your original stake clearly, preferably both by showing it and stating it, and you can't change your mind either by increasing it – except of course by buying another card – or decreasing it!

It is clear, I hope, that the banker pays out an amount equal to the stake to each player whose cards are better than his: pontoon being the best hand, followed by the five-card trick, 21 other than a pontoon (e.g. Ten, Five, and Six), 20, 19, 18, 17, 16. And, of course, if he 'goes bust', he pays each player with a valid hand. He takes the stakes of players who bust, or have worse hands than his, or whose hands are equal to his – this last is what gives the banker his advantage.

Now for the variations, which bring pontoon into the category of hard gambling. If so decided, the banker has the option, having seen his first card – if for example it is an Ace, or even a Ten or a court card – of saying 'Double up'. This means that to stay in play the players have to double their stakes: more for them if they win, or more to lose if the banker wins.

Again, if it is so decided at the start, the banker who has a pontoon receives just the stake from a player who also has a pontoon, double the stake from a player with 'five and under', and treble the stake from other players. If he has 21 (not with a pontoon) or a five-card trick, he receives a single stake from players with similar hands and double from the others. If he decides to stick on 19 for example, he takes the single stake from players with 19 or less, but pays double stakes to players with 21 or 'five and under'.

And he pays single stakes, as in the basic system, when no special combinations are held by anyone.

One more thing: if a player does not wish to take the bank he can sell his chance to the highest bidder. But as it is usually profitable to be banker, and such good fun, always take the chance.

I learnt this game when I was in the Army on guard duty – during the time I was off watch, of course! Be warned when you play pontoon for high stakes, especially with strangers – be on your guard. It's a wonderful party game for small stakes; not much actual skill about it, a big element of luck, but still plenty of scope for judgement. Different 'schools' have slightly different rules – for example, some people allow the splitting of tens and courts cards, some allow you to split any two cards of similar value – but nothing you can't easily understand right away.

NAP

Required: 1 pack of 52 cards

Five cards are dealt to each player (from two to six persons can play comfortably), so there are always cards left over, and it is this fact that makes Nap the excellent game it is.

Nap is rather like small-scale Solo Whist. In Solo, however, all the pack is dealt, so the high cards have their full value. In Nap, because there are always undealt cards still in the pack and no one knows which they are, there is no way of knowing the true value of those held by the players. It may be, for example, that the Nine of Spades is unbeatable because all the higher Spades are still in the pack.

It is unfortunate, however, that the player who holds such a valuable card is unaware of its potential!

Players cut for deal, highest card cut taking the deal. In subsequent games the deal passes clockwise round the table in the usual way. Five cards are dealt to each player one at a time, and the rest of the pack is put face down on the table.

Having looked at your hand you try to assess its value, and in doing so you bear in mind that on account of those unknown cards in the pack your cards may have a greater value than usual. Whether they have or not is the gamble you are obliged to take.

First player to call is the one on the dealer's left. The calls, in ascending order, are two, three, *misère,* four, and Nap: meaning that you undertake to make two tricks, three tricks, no tricks at all, four tricks, and all five tricks respectively. If you do not wish to call, you pass.

If your call wins, i.e. is the highest made, the first card you lead denotes the trump suit, except in *misère* when there are no trumps. And the player who has made the highest call leads.

Players call, overcall, or pass in turn, but, of course, if someone calls Nap there can be no further calls.

If your call holds good, try straight away to make your tricks. Keep the lead if you can. No messing about, lead your highest trump card because you want to know at once just what cards your opponents have. If for example you went Nap with four Hearts, King high, plus a King of Clubs: lead your King of Hearts and hold your breath, hoping that no one has the Ace. If the King takes the trick you can breathe again.

108

The chance of there being an Ace against you differs in proportion to the number of players taking part. Should there be two of you, the odds are that your opponent does not have the Ace; on the other hand, if there are six players it is more than an even chance that one of them holds it. So, you see, your judgement must be on a sliding scale.

Remember also that you are on your own, the others are all against you. There is no need for one opponent to beat another; once your lead has been beaten the others can play low, or discard if they cannot follow suit.

As in all trump games, even the worst trump beats the highest card of any other suit.

If there are several players you are happy in the knowledge that the trumps are likely to be more or less divided between them. If you hold four trumps, the other players perhaps hold one or two each, if that. So with your first lead you may draw all, or most of, what trumps are against you. The same applies of course to the other suits. But there is always the chance of a freak distribution – that's the fun of the game.

Whether your call is nap, or two, three, or four, the strategy is the same: make your tricks as quickly as you can while you have the lead. If you lose the lead, on, say, a call of three, you cannot rely on an opponent leading a card you can take – unless of course you have small trumps to take care of a lead in a suit you have none of.

Calling and playing *misère* is much the same in Solo Whist, except that you may be able to take greater chances; you have more chance of throwing away a high card when you cannot follow suit. You need a Two or a Three for your lead; and even that is no certainty, especially with only one or two opponents, because they may be unable to follow suit.

Nap is played for small stakes as a rule; settlement is immediate. You can use counters or matches and agree their value, but it is easiest to use plenty of small change.

The successful caller collects the value of his call from each other player, two units for two, three for three, four for four; and three for *misère,* but ten for Nap. If he loses he pays each opponent the same, but only six units for Nap.

There is not much else to say about this game, though regular players who become very expert might have much to add. It is a rattling good game, and if you have only a short time available

– ten minutes in the lunch-hour – it's still worth while getting the cards out. I know that Nap is short for Napoleon; but I wonder why it was called after him.

CHINESE FAN-TAN

Required: 1 pack of cards, marked sheet of paper, "chips" (counters or matches)

As many players as you please; a pack of cards; a good-sized card or piece of paper marked like this:

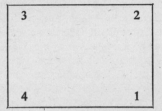

This, I am led to believe, is the original game of Fan-Tan. The Chinese of old always had the reputation of being heavy gamblers: they would bet on two flies moving up a wall.

You bet with money, or counters, or matches. In the middle of the table is a card or paper with the numbers 1, 2, 3, and 4 in the corners as shown. This can be made in a moment and then you are in business.

Bets can be placed in any of eight positions: on the numbers in the corners, or in the middle of the sides between the numbers.

Bets in the corners win if that actual number turns up, and the banker pays out 3 to 1. Bets between numbers win if either of those two numbers turn up, and the punter is paid even money.

Players cut for bank, the lowest card cut taking it. After each game the bank moves round the table to the left, i.e. clockwise.

The game, if you can call it a game, begins. The pack is shuffled (why, I don't know) and placed in front of the banker. He cuts the pack into two heaps and picks up the lower portion. Then he deals this portion into four piles until:

(a) No cards are left, in which case 4 wins.
(b) One card is left, in which case 1 wins.
(c) Two cards are left, in which case 2 wins.
(d) Three cards are left, in which case 3 wins.
It's as simple as that. It is just a gamble.

111

BLIND HOOKEY
Required: 1 pack of cards, 'chips' (counters or matches)

This is a very simple, fairly old, little, gambling game. Decide beforehand on the stakes, in cash or using counters or matches to represent cash.

Any number can play. Cut for deal, highest card deals, Ace high. The deal goes round the table to the left in turn.

The pack is shuffled and cut. The dealer proceeds to deal five cards each to as many persons as may be playing.

These little packets are placed face down in front of the players and not looked at. The game begins.

Each player except the dealer must make a guess; he places a unit stake either on the left or the right of his little packet.

If the stake is placed to the left of the packet, it means that the player gambles that his top card is higher than the top card of the dealer's packet; if to the right, it indicates that he thinks it will be lower in value than the dealer's.

When all players have ruminated and placed their bets, the dealer makes his first move by turning the top card of his packet face up. Then one by one in strict rotation the other players turn over their top cards.

All players who have predicted correctly receive payment equal to their stake. The dealer takes the stakes off all who have guessed wrongly – and also those of players whose cards are equal in value to his.

In this way the game continues until the five cards each have been turned up, when you shuffle the pack and have a fresh deal. If you enjoyed that little session you will probably carry on into the early hours.

RED DOG

Required: 1 pack of cards, 'chips' (counters or matches)

This is a simple family gambling game, generally known in America as High-Card Pool. Any number up to ten can play.

Players cut for deal, highest card cut taking the first deal. From then on the deal passes clockwise round the table.

Use money, counters, or my famous matches to bet with. Fix a limit for bets beforehand, say five units. Each player puts two matches (or whatever your units are) into the kitty (or pot, or pool) in the middle of the table to start with. Any time the kitty is exhausted, or gets very low, all players 'chip in' with another two to replenish it.

The pack is shuffled and cut. The dealer deals five cards to each player, face down, and places the balance of the pack in front of him. If ten are playing, the balance is only two cards, of course. No matter.

The players pick up their cards and examine them. What they have to assess is the chance that they hold a card of the same suit as the unknown card on top of the pack (i.e. the balance of the pack) but higher in value.

Then in turn, starting with the player on the dealer's left, they place their stakes in front of them. Everyone must bet at least one unit, and if you hold low cards, and one or more suits are missing from your hand, one will be quite enough to bet.

If, however, you have fairly high cards in all four suits you will consider your chance good and bet the limit. Clever players have a way of working out the chances mathematically so that they know just how much to bet; but unless you are playing for big money it's hardly worth going to all that trouble.

In America, by the way, they don't usually fix a limit, but any player can bet up to the total amount in the kitty.

When all bets have been made the dealer turns the top card of the balance of the pack face up. A player who has a higher card (Ace is high) of the same suit receives an amount equal to his stake from the kitty. All losing bets go into the kitty.

Then you start again, the first player taking the deal and the pack being assembled, shuffled and cut as before.

Quite a good little game.

NEWMARKET

Required: 1 pack of 52 cards, A, K, Q, J, from a second pack,
'chips' (counters or matches)

As you would expect from the name, Newmarket is primarily a
gambling game; there is little scope for skill, so much depending
on the luck of the deal. A certain amount of judgement is called
for, and it is important to remember what cards have been
played.

But it is a jolly party game for four, five or six players. If you
play for actual money you would need lots of small change, and
you could soon run into quite large sums; so I suggest using
poker chips, or counters, or of course matches. Let someone act
as banker and sell counters to the players at five or ten a penny,
at the start, and buy them back afterwards.

You need a pack of fifty-two cards, plus an Ace, King, Queen
and Jack from another pack, of different suits. These are called
the 'luxuries' and are placed face up in the middle of the table.
Before each deal the players place bets on these cards, up to an
agreed maximum of say five counters: they can plunge on one
card, or divide their stakes between two or three or all four.

Cut for deal, lowest card taking the deal; subsequently the
deal passes round to the left in the usual way. The pack needs to
be well shuffled after each game, by the way. Cards are dealt
singly to each player and to a dummy hand, which is left face
downwards and is not seen. Odd cards remaining after the deal
are added to the dummy. So with four players they would get
ten cards each, and there would be twelve in the dummy; five
players, eight each and again twelve for the dummy; six players,
seven each and ten in the dummy.

You can vary this arrangement if you wish: with five players,
for example, you could deal nine each and seven to dummy.
Decide at the start, and stick to it.

There are two objects in the play of the cards. First, to play
any card or cards which you have in your hand which matches
one of the 'luxury' cards, when you immediately collect all the
stakes which have been placed on that card. Secondly, to 'go
out', i.e. to play all the cards in your hand, before any other
player does so. To the player who goes out first, each other
player pays one counter for each card he still holds. Just one
other thing to tell you: stakes on the luxury cards which have

not been won remain there for the next deal. This can sometimes happen for several consecutive deals, and the stakes can
mount up to quite an appreciable amount, which makes it all
more exciting.

In the play, Aces rank high, and other cards in their usual
order; there are no trumps.

The player to the dealer's left leads. He can select any suit,
but may lead only the lowest card he holds of that suit. The
player who holds the next higher card of that suit plays it, and
so on, until there is a 'stop': naturally the Ace of the suit is a
'stop', but so is any card if the next higher happens to be in the
unseen dummy. After playing a stop card the same player leads
again, in the same suit or a different one, as he wishes; again, the
lowest card.

To see how all this works out, let's shuffle a pack and deal out
hands for a five-player game. From another pack we first set
out the luxuries, the Ace of Spades, King of Hearts, Queen of
Diamonds, Jack of Clubs. Let's assume that player A stakes 5
on the QD; B places 3 on the KH and 2 on the QD; C stakes 2
on the JC and 1 on each of the others; D puts 3 on the AS
and 1 each on the KH and QD; E stakes 4 on the JC and 1 on
the AS.

Now we deal. A receives, Spades: Ace; Hearts: 5, 4; Diamonds: Jack, 8, 4; Clubs: 10, 4.

B gets, Spades: 8, 5; Hearts: King, Queen, 3; Diamonds: Ace
and King; Clubs: 5.

C gets, Spades: 7; Hearts: Jack, 9; Diamonds: 10, 7, 6, 5;
Clubs: 9.

D gets, Spades: King, Jack; Hearts: 2; Diamonds: Queen, 9,
2; Clubs: 8, 6.

E gets, Spades: Queen, 10, 9, 6: Hearts: 10; Diamonds: 3;
Clubs: Queen, 2.

And face down in dummy go, Spades: 4, 3, 2; Hearts: Ace, 8,
7, 6; Diamonds: none; Clubs: Ace, King, Jack, 7, 3.

'It's A's lead, and what a lucky chap he is: he holds the Ace of
Spades, which is not only a luxury but also a stop, and he has no
lower Spades. If he had, he would have had to lead the lowest;
as it is, he jumps at the chance of playing his Ace. He immediately collects the 5 counters staked on it, and after his stop
he leads again. He has no other luxuries to lead up to, so he
plays his two constructive Hearts, first the 4, then the 5.

Though he didn't know it, the 6 is in dummy, so his 5 is a stop. His lead again; he plays the 4D. C plays his 5, 6 and 7. A plays the 8D, D the 9D, C the 10D, A the JD, D the QD – a luxury – and collects the 9 counters staked on it, a nice little pick-up.

B play the KD and AD, a stop of course. He leads the 3H, knowing that it is a stop as the 4 has gone. So now he can play his QH and KH, collecting the 5 counters from its corresponding luxury. No one produces the Ace, because of course it is in dummy; so it's his lead again, and he selects the 5S.

E plays the 6, C the 7, B the 8 (doing fine, only his 5C to play and he's out!), E plays the 9 and 10, D the Jack, E the Queen, D the King – a stop, as the Ace has gone. D remembers that his 2H is a stop, and plays it; then his 6C, which turns out to be another stop, the 7 being in dummy; then his 8C.

A plays his 10C, reluctant as he is to give someone the chance of playing the JC, a luxury. No need to worry: the JC is in dummy. So A plays his 4C, and he is out. Note that he was able to play his 10 before the 4 as he was following another player's lead; if he had led Clubs, he would have had to play the 4 first.

So A, who has already picked up 5 counters from the luxury AS, collects a counter from B, who has only one card left, 2 from C, 1 from D, and 4 from E, who is the biggest loser in this deal. D is also on the right side, thanks to his nice pick-up on the Queen of Diamonds.

The stakes remain on the Jack of Clubs. The players again place their bets on the luxuries, the cards are collected and well shuffled, and it's A's deal and B's lead.

Now, that deal worked out pretty well. But sometimes the cards fall in such a way that one player gets most of the play – and cashes in. I have just shuffled and dealt again, and this is what happened. Let's assume that the players made their stakes exactly as before.

A (dealer) gets, Spades: none; Hearts: Queen, 10, 8, 6, 4; Diamonds: 10; Clubs: King, 5.

B gets, Spades: King, Jack, 7; Hearts: Ace, 3; Diamonds: none; Clubs: 6, 3, 2.

C gets, Spades: Ace, Queen, 9, 2; Hearts: none; Diamonds: 9; Clubs: Ace, Jack, 9.

116

D gets, Spades: none; Hearts: Jack; Diamonds: 7, 6, 3; Clubs: Queen, 10, 8, 7.

E gets, Spades: 5, 4; Hearts: King, 9, 5; Diamonds: Ace, King; Clubs: 4.

The other 12 cards are in dummy, of course. Looking at the hands, could you forecast the winner?

Well, B leads, then plays 3C. E plays the 4, A the 5, B the 6, D the 7 and 8, C the 9, D the 10, C the Jack (collecting the 12 counters that are on it), D the Queen, A the King, C the Ace, a stop of course.

C leads the 2S, which turns out to be a stop. He leads the 9S, also a stop. He leads the QS. B plays the KS. C plays the AS, collecting 5; it's a stop; he leads the 9D and is out.

So C, who has already picked up 17 counters from luxuries, collects 6 from A, 5 from B, 4 from D, and 7 from E: total 39, not bad for a stake of 5.

Stakes on the King of Hearts and Queen of Diamonds remain there, a nice little nest-egg for the next game. B collects the cards and shuffles them preparatory to dealing, and off we go again.

You'll enjoy Newmarket; but keep the stakes low, unless you really want to go in for heavy gambling.

In the USA, Newmarket is known as Michigan, or Chicago, or Boodle, or Stops; and they play it slightly differently. But I think that our name, and our rules, are better.

Games for the young

GAMES FOR THE YOUNG

Give an old pack to a toddler, and he will play happily for hours. Teach older ones how to make card castles, and you will have peace for hours.

The card games suitable for the very young are surely known to everyone, or should be: but just in case, I feel that I must include details of a few.

BEGGAR MY NEIGHBOUR
Required: 1 pack of cards

Or 'Beat Your Neighbour Out of Doors', or 'Strip Jack Naked'.

My dear mama taught me this game goodness knows how many years ago, and for young children it is the best card game. I know. It is simplest for two players, and any old pack can be used, even an incomplete one; for three or more it is best to use two packs mixed up together.

If there are just the two of you the procedure is quite simple. Shuffle the pack and divide into two halves, as nearly as you can judge; give the little monster one half while you keep the other.

Decide who shall play first: monster decides that he will, so he turns up the top cards and places it face up on the surface whatever it may be.

If it is a pip card you turn up your top card and place it face up on to his. So you go on in turn until one or other of you turns up a picture card or an Ace.

Then the other player has to 'pay' so many cards: one for a Jack, two for a Queen, three for a King, four for an Ace. If the payment is completed in pip cards the winner takes the pile, turns it face down and tucks it away under his other cards, and continues to play as before.

But if, before the payment is completed, another picture card or Ace turns up, the debt is wiped out and the other player has to start paying. So the game continues until one of the players has won all the cards, and you shuffle and start again.

When there are more than two players, all turn up cards in

120

turn going clockwise round the table. When one turns up a picture card or Ace it is the next player in turn who has to do the paying. If the payment is completed in pip cards the one who turned up the picture card or Ace takes the pile; if before it is completed a picture card or Ace turns up, then it is again the next player who has to start paying. All cards are, of course, played on to one pile in the middle of the table.

It is all very exciting; of course the Jacks are the most useful cards to hold because they need payment of only one card, and this is usually pretty safe.

For young children this is the greatest, and lasts for hours.

SNAP

Required: 1 or 2 packs of cards

Played with any old pack, and if there are more than three players two packs can be shuffled together. As with the last game, it doesn't matter much if a few cards are missing.

Whether two are playing or more, the procedure is the same. Having shared out the cards equally, either by dealing or by guesswork, the players turn their cards face up one by one, simultaneously. The moment two players produce cards of the same value, 'Snap' is shouted: the first player to say 'Snap' takes the loser's face-up pile of cards.

This noisy and most amusing game continues until one player has 'snapped' all the cards and is proclaimed the winner. Then it begins all over again.

MUGGINS

Required: 1 old pack of 52 cards, at least 4 players

Here is a really jolly party game which I found in an old Victorian book. I doubt if it has been described in print these last sixty or seventy years. It is decidedly a game for the Very Young; in fact, if everyone plays cautiously and carefully there's not much point in it.

Until a few minutes ago, just as I began to write this section, I did not know anyone who had ever heard of Muggins. But a friend rang me up on the phone, and in the course of conversation happened to ask me what I was doing. When I told him, he said: 'Good heavens, I thought that only our family played Muggins. My grandmother taught it to me when I was a very little boy.'

You need an old pack of 52 cards, and at least four or five players. The more the merrier; and if more than seven or eight are playing, use two packs shuffled together.

Someone deals the cards round, one at a time, face down, and the surplus cards at the end are turned face up in the middle of the table for Mugginses. With four players, they would have twelve cards each and there would be four Mugginses; with five players, ten each and two Mugginses; with six players, eight each and four Mugginses, and so on.

Players tidy their cards into a face-down pile in front of them without looking at them. Then starting with the player on the dealer's left, in turn they turn the top card face up a little nearer the centre of the table. The object is to play off all your cards. The one who does so first is the winner.

You get rid of them by placing them face up on any other face-up card on the table with which they are in an ascending or descending sequence. Suits don't matter, just the values; but Ace is low. So you can play a Queen on to an exposed King, or Jack; a Seven on to an exposed Eight, or Six. But you can't play an Ace on to a King, or a King on to an Ace.

The first player, of course, has only the central Mugginses to go at. But as play goes round the table there are more and more exposed cards to go at, at the top of the players' face-up piles. And you have to keep an eye on them all.

Now, you have to observe certain rules of precedence. If possible you place your card on to one of the central Muggins piles. If that is not possible, then on to one of the other players' piles. And if there are more than one players' piles on to which you could go, you have to use the one nearest to you on your left.

As soon as a player spots another player breaking a rule, he shouts 'Muggins', and the other players take up the cry. Then the offending player has to accept one card from each other player – the top cards of their face-down piles – which he places underneath his own pile.

So, if you place a card on top of your own face-up pile which could have gone elsewhere, or on to a player's pile when it could have gone on to one of the central Muggins piles, or on to another player's pile when it could have gone on to the pile of a player nearer to you on your left, you're a Muggins yourself and suffer the penalty.

As soon as a player's face-down pile is exhausted, he turns his face-up pile over and starts again.

If one player is persistently slow, carefully examining all the face-up cards before playing a card, it rather spoils the fun. There are two ways of dealing with this contingency. One is for all the other players to start a chant of 'Hurry up, hurry up' which will probably confuse the offender into making a mistake. The other is to allow, say, a ten-second time limit; if there happens to be an electric clock with a large centre seconds hand in the room, one player could be appointed as timekeeper. Or the timekeeper could have a watch with a seconds hand, or just count aloud. And the slowcoach could be declared a Muggins.

But don't make the game too formal: after all, it's only fun. Perhaps the 'hurry up' idea is the best, to be adopted only if it's really needed.

Last word: if you are a grown-up playing with the young-sters, don't be too alert. Allow yourself to be a Muggins now and again, which will give great pleasure to the children. But be careful not to let them suspect that you are not trying your best.

PELMANISM
Required: 1 or 2 packs of cards

I have a vague idea, which I cannot verify, that this game was included in the Pelman Course, which had quite a vogue about fifty years ago, as a memory-training exercise. But it became popular, played just for fun, among people who had never heard of Mr Pelman and his course.

The game is sometimes known as Concentration or simply The Memory Test. And it is very suitable for inclusion in this section because quite young children often prove to be extraordinarily good at it; in fact they are apt to put their elders to shame by consistently wiping the floor with them.

Any number can play, up to ten or so. Perhaps for a larger number you could use two packs shuffled together, but you would need a very big table.

Pelmanism is easily learnt. Shuffle the pack thoroughly and lay out all the cards face down in the middle of the table. Somebody starts by turning two cards face up at random. If they match, that is, if they are two Kings, or two Sixes, or whatever, the player takes them and has another try. When he fails to turn up two matching cards they are turned face down again in their original positions and the turn passes to the next player going clockwise round the table. When all the cards have been taken, the player who has collected most cards is the winner. That's all there is to it.

But it's more fun than you might think from this bald description. You try to remember what cards the others turn up and exactly where they are. So when the first card you turn up is, say, a Jack, you remember that someone else a few turns ago had a Jack which he failed to match and you rack your brains to think where it was. That's where young people are so good: they seem to have more photographic memories than us. And very often when it gets down to the last dozen cards or so smart youngsters will clear the table.

One word of warning. Use a clean, fairly new pack. Otherwise some cards soon become recognizable by spots on the back, or small creases, and that gives an unfair advantage to someone who is familiar with that particular pack.

BANGO

Required: 1 or 2 packs of cards, sweets for prizes

A jolly party game for youngsters, for three, four of five players plus a non-playing 'caller'. Have a box of chocolates, or a bag of wrapped sweets, or a tube of Smarties handy, so that the winner of each game gets one sweet as a prize.

The game is a simplified version of Bingo played with nothing more than a pack of cards, and so much less trouble. The caller having shuffled the pack deals out five cards to each player, which are placed face up in front of them. Then he turns up the rest of the cards one at a time, calling its value. A player who has a card of the same value turns it face down, and the first to have turned down all his cards and to shout 'Bango' gets the prize.

If you want to take a little more trouble and make the game a bit more precise, divide the pack into red and black cards beforehand, dealing one colour to the players and using the other for calling. And if there are more than five players, do the same with two packs.

Bango is a lot of fun.

DONKEY
Required: 1 pack of cards (not new!), sweets for prizes

You need a good supply of Smarties, or some other small-sized sweets, for this game too. At the start of each deal place one less sweet than there are players in the middle of the table – on a plate, for the sake of hygiene, if you like.

And before you start, sort out from the pack as many sets of four cards of the same denomination – four Aces, four Twos, and so on – as there are players, and put the rest of the pack on one side. Shuffle the sets well together, and deal them round, four cards to each player.

The idea is to collect a set of four matching cards. As soon as a player succeeds he drops his cards and grabs a sweet; the others follow suit as quickly as possible, and the slowest, the one left without a sweet, is the 'donkey'.

Then you replenish the supply, shuffle the cards, and deal again.

So, the deal completed, players look at their cards and decide what to collect: obviously, if you start with two or three alike you go for those. One player, or the supervising grown-up, calls 'Pass'. And simultaneously each player passes one card face downwards to the player on his left. As soon as they have time to look at their cards 'Pass' is called again, and so it goes until someone has four alike. No one is allowed to look at the card he is receiving until he has passed one of his on; that's cheating, and so is 'going out' without having a set of four. Cheating is penalized by being made a 'double Donkey' and getting no sweet while the others receive two each.

Donkey is an ideal game for using up an old pack of which one or two cards have been lost or damaged. Don't play it with a nice new expensive pack: the cards get horribly sticky in no time, and if the grown-ups try to play bridge with it later they won't be at all pleased.

127

SNIP-SNAP-SNORUM
Required: 1 pack of cards

I suppose that it is the funny name, and the funny effect of the words the players call as they play their cards, that makes me think of this as a game for children. No real skill is required, though a certain degree of judgement – which a bright youngster will soon pick up – can make all the difference between winning and losing.

A full pack of cards is needed, and from four to seven players is the ideal number. The cards are shuffled and dealt as usual.

The player to the dealer's left leads any card, saying 'Snip'. The player who holds the next highest card plays it and says 'Snap'. The player who has the next highest plays it and says 'Snorum'. The player who has the next highest plays it and says 'Hi cockalorum'. Finally the player who holds the next highest card plays it and says 'Jig'. That completes the sequence and the player who called 'Jig' begins a new one, leading a card and saying 'Snip'; so it goes on.

The 'Jig' card is always a stop. But so is a King, because the cards rank from Ace, lowest, upwards to King. So having played a King, whether it was a 'Snorum' or a 'Hi cockalorum' or even a 'Snip', that player must start a new sequence with a 'Snip'.

I omitted to say that players must follow suit – or did you realize that? Anyhow, if the Six of Diamonds, say, is led as 'Snip', it is followed by the Seven, 'Snap', the Eight, 'Snorum', the Nine, 'Hi cockalorum', and the Ten of Diamonds will complete the sequence with 'Jig'. So the player who 'jigged' will start afresh with any card of the same or a different suit.

As the game proceeds more and more cards become stops. If, as above, a sequence has started with the Six of Diamonds, and later someone leads the Two of Diamonds, then the Five will be a stop card at 'Hi cockalorum'.

The object of the game is to get rid of all your cards, and the player who does so first is the winner. So obviously it pays to play as many stop cards as possible.

This is where the strategy comes in, and as I say, an intelligent youngster will soon get the idea. Suppose you find in your hand, say, the Four, Five, Seven, and Nine of Hearts. You would not lead the Four, because someone else would 'Jig' with the Eight. No: you would lead the Five, come in at 'Snorum' with the Seven, and 'Jig' with the Nine. What's more, when another player led a low Heart your Four would be a stop card, the Five having gone.

I came across 'Snip-Snap-Snorum' in two scarce Victorian books of games; they gave slightly different versions but I think this is the better of the two. It must be quite an old card game. I think it is too good to be forgotten; it could become a favourite with your young people.

OLD MAID
Required: 1 pack of cards

Or Slippery Lizzie: but not to be confused with Black Maria, which is alternatively called Slippery Ann. I have not included the latter in this book because I am not very fond of it; but Old Maid is definitely for the very young.

Take the Queen of Clubs from the pack and put it aside. (Don't forget where you put it, though, because you will want the pack complete another time.)

The corresponding card of the same colour, the Queen of Spades, is the Old Maid and the simple object of the game is to avoid being left with her. Because, in the case of a young lady, this would signify that she was destined to become an Old Maid, a fate too dreadful to contemplate: and in the case of a young man, that he would have an Old Maid for his girl friend, which would be even worse.

The remaining fifty-one cards are dealt between the players in the ordinary way. Unless there are three players they won't go round evenly, but as subsequent deals pass round the table any inequalities even themselves out.

The players examine their cards and look out for pairs, which are placed face down on the table. It should be decided beforehand whether any two cards of like value may be paired, i.e. two Fours, two Jacks, and so on; or like cards of the same colour, which prolongs the game somewhat.

Pairs having been taken out of the hands, each player fans his remaining cards face down to his left-hand neighbour who picks out one card. If it pairs with one of his cards the pair is placed down as before, and again the hands are offered for a card to be taken. This procedure continues as the players run out of cards, until the last pair goes down, and one unfortunate person is left with the Old Maid.

There is perhaps a little scope for cunning in the matter of whereabouts, if you are trying to get rid of the Queen of Spades, you place it in the fan of cards which you offer to your neighbour. It might be worth trying, to make some other card look pretty prominent so that he will think that is the one to avoid, and actually have the Old Maid less conspicuously placed a card or two away to his right of it – or his left if he is left-handed. I'll let you into a secret – this is a technique which magicians sometimes adopt.

CHASE THE ACE

Required: 1 pack of cards, counters (or sweets)

This is a very simple no-skill game suitable for young people. It is rarely described in books on card games so you may like to learn it, which won't take you long.

Up to eight or nine can play. You use a pack of 52 cards. Each player to start with is given three counters – or matches or, as I have suggested elsewhere, Smarties or wrapped sweets. When he has lost his three 'lives' he is out of the game, and the winner is the last survivor.

Dealer deals one card to each player, face down, and for the moment no one looks at his card. The object is to avoid holding the lowest card. King is high and Ace low, and the suits rank as in Bridge: Spades highest, then Hearts, then Diamonds, and Clubs lowest. So the Ten of Hearts is higher than the Ten of Diamonds, and the Six of Clubs is higher than the Five of Spades.

First player, on the dealer's left, looks at his card. If it is a King he places it face upwards in front of him. Otherwise he can either 'stand', and say so, or exchange his card with that of the player on his left. The next player does likewise, and so on round the table.

When the turn comes round to the dealer, he can either 'stand' or exchange his card for the top card of the pack in front of him.

Then all cards are turned face up, and whoever holds the lowest puts a counter into the kitty. The player who was at the dealer's left gathers up the cards, places them at the bottom of the pack, and deals afresh.

And that's all there is to Chase the Ace.

Patience games

PATIENCE, OR SOLITAIRE
Required: 1 'patience' set, or 1 or 2 packs of cards

I have always enjoyed playing Patience, and honestly, I must have played it for many hundreds of hours during my lifetime.

Patience or Solitaire, as the latter name implies, is usually a game for one, but there are exceptions. Patience is the English name; Solitaire is what it is called in America. In this country, Solitaire is a one-person game played on a board with marbles or pegs.

As certain principles and terms are used in a number of different Patience games, it will save repetition if I explain them before we start.

Foundations are cards set out face up at the beginning of the game, on which piles of other cards are built up in sequence according to the particular game.

Sequences may be *ascending*, i.e. Ace, 2, 3, etc. from the bottom upwards, or 6, 7, 8, etc., and may go 'round the corner' as Queen, King, Ace, 2, 3, etc. Or *descending*, ie. King, Queen, Jack, etc., or 8, 7, 6, etc., or 3, 2, Ace, King, Queen, etc.

A *tableau* (or *depot*) is a layout of single cards or piles of cards on to which cards may be played from the pack, or stock, and from which cards may be transferred to build up the foundations; cards may in some games be transferred singly or in sequences from one part of the tableau to another.

The *stock* is the balance of the pack from which cards are played, or a pile of cards available for use.

The *talon* is the pile formed of unplayed cards from the stock; these cards may be lost, or used when the stock is exhausted, according to the particular game.

Spaces occur when the whole of a pile from the tableau has been transferred to the foundations; they can be filled with a card from the stock.

Exposed cards are those not covered or overlapped by other cards and therefore available for play.

With a few exceptions, cards once built on to the foundations cannot be removed, but those built on to the tableau can be transferred.

I am going to explain a number of different Patience games, the ones out of all the hundreds which have been invented that I feel you will get the most fun from; and I would like to begin with one given to me by my magician friend, Patrick Page, which he calls 'Dundee'.

Required: 1 pack of cards, with Jokers

You won't even need a table to play on for this game. By the way, I recommend the use of the special small Patience cards which can be bought almost anywhere; they don't take up half as much room as full-sized cards and are fascinating to play with.

Shuffle the pack thoroughly, and give it a cut. Just one thing: when playing Patience, it is essential that you do not cheat. You would be amazed to find how many people do, in order to have the joy of seeing a patience game 'come out'. If you cheat, you only spoil it for yourself; so let's have a bit of self-discipline, please.

Back to Dundee. Having mixed the cards well, hold the pack in your left hand in the dealing position.

You can do the following silently, or as loudly as you like.

You are about to deal the cards one by one face up on to your lap, on the seat beside you, into an upturned hat, or on to a table. But before you deal each card face up, say a value, for example King. If the card is a King the game is over and you have to start again. You try *not* to predict the card correctly, and you get as far through the pack as you can without naming any card accurately.

I have tried to do this and have not yet managed to deal right through the pack; it is quite amazing how impossible it is, it's almost like a conjuring trick. What a terrific party game this would make.

Now try it the other way round: see how many cards you can predict correctly. Who knows – you may be a natural clairvoyant!

Just one point: you do not have to say Jack of Diamonds, Three of Spades, and so on. Just say Jack, Three, Ten, etc.

If you live alone and play this game it could start you talking to yourself – so please be careful!

32/5

136

Required: 1 Pack of 52 cards, a fair-sized table

This is a good game with a fair chance of going out, i.e. completing it. Shuffle the pack and deal out your tableau as follows:

Deal nine cards face up in a row. Directly under this row starting from the left deal eight cards in a row. It will conserve space if you overlap the first row by about three-quarters of the card. Then starting from the left again deal seven in the next row, and so on until you reach the last 'row' of one card: that is forty-five face-up cards in all. The seven cards left over are placed in a separate face-up row to form the stock, called the Belgian Reserve.

These seven, and the nine cards at the bottom of the columns on the tableau, are the only ones which are 'free' to be played. Any free card which is an Ace must be placed above the tableau as a foundation, upon which you build in the same suit in ascending order.

You also build in descending order, any suits but alternate colours, on the bottom cards of the columns of the tableau, as in most Patience games. But there is one important difference from most Patience games: only one card may be moved at a time. You cannot transfer a sequence *en bloc* in this game.

So you have to make use of spaces. A space occurs when an entire column has been cleared by transferring its cards one at a time to other columns or to the foundations, and of course the columns of only one, two, three, or four cards at the right-hand side of the tableau are usually the first to be cleared.

When you have a space you can move an exposed card into it from the tableau in order to free the next card for transfer or building on. Or you can fill it with a card from the stock on which you can build.

Spaces are invaluable and the cunning use of them is the secret of playing this particular variety of Patience. If you can contrive to have two vacant spaces you can juggle about: for example, say you have a red Eight exposed in one column, with a black Seven and a red Ten behind it. In another column the exposed card is a black Nine with a card you want to free behind it. Now, if you put the red Eight on to the black Nine, and the black Seven on to the red Eight, you cannot as in most games transfer the 9–8–7 sequence on to the Ten – so the sequence blocks the cards you want. If, however, you put the red Eight into a space, the black Seven into another space, transfer the black Nine on to the red Ten, then the red Eight on to the black Nine, and the black Seven on to the red Eight, now the card you want is exposed and you have your two spaces back for further use.

Three vacant spaces at a time, or even four, give you still more scope. So the important thing in this game is to think carefully how you can make the best use of them; don't lose a space even temporarily if you can avoid it. Remember that if you have to move a King into a vacant space you have lost the use of that space until the end of the game when you don't need it any more anyhow.

Similarly, conserve your reserve stock cards until you really need them to make progress, don't build with them just for the sake of building because once they have been taken out of stock they cannot be put back. You can, however, move a card – the top card, of course – from a foundation on to the tableau if it will help.

A last word about strategy. Try to build up the foundations evenly, either all four, or at least one black and one red. Don't rush to build up just one. Don't build up long sequences in the tableau; remember that all those cards will have to be moved one at a time to free cards behind them. The ideal thing is to have sequences in the columns with no low cards behind them; and if towards the end of the game you have most of the pack arranged in sequence in four columns, you are laughing, because then you can transfer to the foundations without any hold-ups.

But the best way to learn the strategy is to play the game with thought and – well, patience!

King Albert is a very good Patience game.

CALCULATION (*Le Calcul*)
Required: 1 pack of 52 cards, a table

Remove from the pack any Ace, Deuce, Three, and Four and place them in a row as in the illustration below. Actually, these are the foundations in modern terminology.

The rest of the cards are held ready for dealing. As you turn up cards, you may put them on the foundations (the Ace, Two, Three, and Four) in the following manner:

On the Ace you build upwards in an ascending sequence regardless of suit: Ace, 2, 3, 4, 5, 6, 7, 8, 9, 10, 11 (Jack), 12 (Queen), 13 (King), and stop with the King.

On the Deuce you build upwards BUT in steps of two at a time: 2, 4, 6, 8, 10, 12 (Queen), Ace, 3, 5, 7, 9, 11 (Jack), 13 (King), and stop there.

On the Three you build upwards BUT in steps of three at a time: 3, 6, 9, 12 (Queen), 2, 5, 8, 11 (Jack), Ace, 4, 7, 10, 13 (King), and stop there.

And on the Four you build upwards BUT in steps of four: 4, 8, 12 (Queen), 3, 7, 11 (Jack), 2, 6, 10, Ace, 5, 9, 13 (King), and stop there.

So turn up the first card and see what you have to play with. If it does not suit any of the foundations, place it face up on a discard heap; there are to be four of these, one under each foundation, forming a tableau – see illustration.

Now it is up to you to feed your discards to any position you please, bearing in mind that you will need certain cards later. You can save one heap just for Kings if you wish; but as you play this game you will begin to see the light.

So you keep on turning up cards from the pack in your hand, and you place them one by one to the best of your ability. As the discard heaps (or tableau) begin to build up, never forget that when there is a suitable card on the top of any heap you may play it on to a foundation – but only the top cards.

You may not transfer cards from one discard heap to another. You really must watch every card and sharpen up your modern computer brain so as not to get those foundations mixed up.

If you are successful and your calculation comes out, try the following:

Pick up the completed foundations like this: heap 4 on top of heap 3, both on heap 2, and the three on heap 1. Turn the pack over and deal the first thirteen cards face down in a row. Now deal the next card on number 2 of the row, the next on number 4, then 6, 8, and so on; when you have covered number 12, back to the beginning of the row on to number 1, then 3, 5, 7, and so on, and finally number 13.

Now start with number 3 of the row and then deal on to every third card in the same way until you reach number 13 the second time round. Now the final deal beginning with a card on number 4 of the row, then every fourth card until you have dealt out the whole pack.

Hey, Presto! when you turn the heaps face up you should reveal four Aces, four Twos, four Threes, and so on – your reputation is made!

9

KLONDIKE
Required: 1 pack of 52 cards, a table

Klondike is the popular name given to this particular game of Patience. For me, it was the first game of its kind I was ever taught; we simply called it Patience. However, Klondike it is, it seems.

This is a very good game, very popular, easy to play and lots of fun.

Shuffle the pack and deal as follows: one card face up and the next six face down in a row, seven in all. Go back to the beginning, miss the face-up card and deal the next card face up overlapping the first face-down card, then the next five face down overlapping the five of the first row. And so on. All this sounds terribly complicated until you look at the illustration.

Well, there they are, exactly as I dealt them.

The Aces become the foundations, the cards on which you eventually build the whole pack if your game 'comes out'. The moment an Ace appears, place it above the layout: then you can build on it in ascending order in the same suit, Two, Three, Four, and so on.

The rest of the pack in your hand becomes the stock. There are two ways of playing and you can choose which you like. As in Demon (p 143) you can push off the cards in threes, turning the batch face up, and using the exposed card – the top card of the face-up batch – if you can. If you can, the next card is exposed and available: if not, turn up a fresh batch of three and so on, and when you have gone through the pack turn it over and start again. If after going through the pack in threes there are one or two cards left these can be turned up singly.

Alternatively, put the stock face down on the table in front of you and turn the cards face up by the side of it one at a time. If you adopt this plan you just go once through the stock and then you have finished.

Survey the scene and begin. The Ace of Spades is immediately put above the layout as a foundation and the card which was underneath it is turned face up.

All the face-up cards in the layout can be built on in descending sequences in alternate colours regardless of suit. So put the black Ten on the red Jack and turn up the face-down card now freed. This happily turns out to be the Two of Spades, so put it on the Ace. This leaves you with an empty space, and spaces can be filled only with Kings: lo and behold! you have a King, so transfer it to the space. Once again you have freed a card; turn it up.

The face-up card of your stock is a red Queen. Put it on to the black King. Now see if there are any other cards you can move; if not, turn over another batch of three cards from the stock, or deal another card from the stock according to which way you are playing.

When it helps, sequences of cards can be moved from one column of the layout to another; but only the whole of the sequence, not part of it. Except, of course, that the lowest card of a sequence can be transferred to a foundation at any time.

So there you have it. You win the game when you have four Kings looking you straight in the eye from the top of the four foundation piles. Then you can look back at them unflinchingly with no cards left and say 'I did that without cheating, not even a little'.

In all Patience games, before you start afresh do be sure to shuffle the pack thoroughly. If you don't, you may be faced with an impossible situation in your next game.

DEMON
Required: 1 pack of 52 cards, a little table space

This is a difficult game to get out. The play is simple, and you need no special intelligence – just 'patience'.

Pack in hand, deal off thirteen cards in one pile and turn it face up. This is your stock.

Alongside the pile, deal a row of four cards face up. Above this row deal one card face up. This one card is the first of four foundations, the cards you build on. If it should be, say, a Seven, then any other Sevens which turn up must be placed alongside the first to be built on in due course.

You build on the foundations in ascending order: on a Seven you would build Eight, Nine, Ten, Jack, Queen, King, Ace, Two, Three, Four, Five, Six – all in the same suit, mind you – and then that foundation would be complete.

You still have the remainder of the pack in your hand. Study the layout. You can build descending sequences on those four cards, in alternate colours irrespective of suit. On a black Six, for example, you could build a red Five, a black Four, a red Three, and so on. Or say you already had a sequence headed by a red Five on which you had built a black Four and a red Three, and a black Six turned up in the layout, then you could transfer the whole sequence of Five, Four and Three on to it. (You can't move part of a sequence, it must be the whole sequence). This would give you an empty space which you would immediately fill with the exposed card of the stock.

You can also transfer the exposed card of the stock on to a sequence when it will help – or, of course, on to a foundation.

You still have that pack in your hand. Push a batch of three cards into your other hand and put this little pile face up on the table. Only the face card can be used, but if you can move it on to a sequence or a foundation that exposes the next card for play, and so on. When you can't play, turn up another batch of three cards on to the first, and so on. So you work through the pack three cards at a time; when you come to the end of the pack and have only one or two cards left you can turn those up singly. Then you pick up the pile, turn it over and start again.

Any time a foundation card appears – a Seven as we have assumed, or whatever it is – move it up to start another foundation.

As you play, building downwards in alternate colours and building the foundations upwards in suits, you keep going through the pack in threes until you have four completed foundations – if you are lucky – or until you find yourself going through the pack without making any move. In that case you have not been successful, and the game is over. Shuffle the pack thoroughly before you start again.

Some players have ways of making the game easier, but I can never see the point of it: if you can't get out without fiddling, then have another go, Joe.

SUPER DEMON
Required: 1 pack of 52 cards, a little table space

I have been unable to find a name for this game of Patience, so for the moment I have called it Super Demon. I decided on this name because I tried it in every spare moment for six weeks before it came out. I am informed that this is a favourite with Ronnie Carroll, the singing star.

The plot is simple, but you must keep your wits about you. After several games you will be able to see formations of cards which will tell you that the game can't go out. If, for example, an Ace is covered by a King of the same suit, you know that you cannot succeed: just stop, shuffle, and start again.

Shuffle the pack thoroughly, hold it in your left hand ready to deal, then deal four cards in a row like this:

Look for cards of the same suit and discard the lowest. You can see that the Two of Spades is lower in value than the Nine of Spades – so take it out of the tableau and discard it. The Jack of Clubs is lower than the King of Clubs – so discard that too.

There are now two spaces, which will be filled on the next deal. Again deal four cards, one on the Nine of Spades, one in the space, one in the other space, and one on the King of Clubs.

Once again discard any cards which are lower in value than others of the same suit, as with the first four. Keep on dealing and discarding in the same way. If you have an Ace on top of a pile and the discards create an empty space, the Ace, but only an Ace, can be moved into it.

The game is to end up with the four Aces in a row. It is very difficult. But it is a great deal of fun, it can be played at speed, and as I say, you soon begin to notice certain combinations of cards which indicate that an 'out' is impossible. So this is more than just a mechanical game of Patience; you must keep your eyes open and your brain alert.

SCRAMBLE
Required: as many packs of old cards as there are players

When I was a boy I spent glorious holidays on my Uncle Jack Moxham's farm at Rustfontein, in East Griqualand, South Africa, and how well I remember those wonderful evenings when around an enormous table in front of a huge maize cob fire, all of us would play Scramble Patience.

It was the maddest, rudest, most exciting, most hilarious card game (if you can call it that) that could ever be played. So I thought that I had something new for you: but it seems that this game, or something like it, is known in this country as Racing Demon or Pounce or some such name. Never mind, probably you have never heard of it: so here is THE family Patience game.

You need a pack of cards per player, but there is just one snag; well, two snags, really.

One: use old packs, because they are going to have a rough time.

Two: the packs must have different back designs or colours. If you are really stuck, mark similar packs on the back with a pen or something, just so that you can tell the difference.

Now you all sit around the table each with enough space in front of him for a Klondike layout (p 141). If you are a long way from the middle of the table, those at the ends may have to kneel on a chair or even stand.

Each player holds a shuffled pack of cards. At a given signal you all get going as fast as you can, laying out for Klondike. Put the remainder of the pack face down in front of you, turn the top card face up and place it beside the stock. Keep both hands free – you will need them.

From this moment you must be all eyes and hands. All Aces must be put into the middle immediately as foundations, and anyone can build on them, so as soon as you put one down someone will be waiting to cover it with a Two of the same suit.

It may be that you have an Ace, Two, and Three of the same suit all exposed and ready to play. You are in trouble. You must pick up the Ace in one hand and the Two in the other, put the Ace down and immediately put your Two on top – a smart player will even manage to put his Two between your Two and

147

the Ace, in a split second – and the moment you have placed the Ace your free hand must move like lightning to get the Three to put it on the Two. In the meantime everything is happening all over the place – do I have to explain further? – phew!

As soon as all movement stops you turn up the top card of your stock to open up more excitement; but this of course is done individually and erratically, not in unison. The middle of the table becomes an indescribable battlefield of arms, hands and cards.

There are two rules. One: you may hold only one card in either hand at any moment. Two: if the game ever becomes static you may point out moves to other players, while you wait to pounce.

Of course, apart from these special rules you all play Klondike in the usual way; and perhaps I should make it clear that you don't build on one another's lay-outs, it's only the foundations that are free for all.

When it is all over and the tumult dies, when you have all gone out or stalemated, the reckoning is made. The cards in the middle, the foundations, are gathered up tidily and turned over, and sorted out into heaps of the same back design, and then these are counted. The player with most cards played on to the foundations is the winner. Then you shuffle your packs and away you go again.

If this is the only game you play after you have read this book, you will have had your money's worth. For me, Scramble Patience will always be a reminder of those wonderful holidays when I was young.

POKER PATIENCE

Required: 1 pack of 52 cards, knowledge of Poker scoring hands

I found this game of Patience in a very old book; and a rattling good game it is too.

You need a pack of 52 cards, and a knowledge of the scoring hands in Poker. It's a game for one, but others, each with a pack, could play at the same time and make a contest of it.

Now you must memorize this lot, or make a list and have it with you for reference – or better still, have this book open at this page.

Royal straight flush: Ace, King, Queen, Jack and Ten of the same suit. Counts 50.

Straight flush: a sequence of five cards of the same suit, e.g. 5, 4, 3, 2, Ace of Hearts, or 9, 8, 7, 6, 5 of Spades. Counts 30.

Fours: four cards of the same value, e.g. four Eights, four Kings, etc. Counts 16. (There's one odd card, of course).

Straight: a sequence of five cards of mixed suits. Counts 12.

Full house: three cards of the same value, and two of another value, e.g. three Jacks and two Sixes. Counts 10.

Threes: three cards of the same value, with two odd cards. Counts 6.

Flush: five cards of the same suit, not in sequence. Counts 5.

Two pairs: two cards of the same value, and another two of a different value, along with an odd card, e.g. two Sixes, two Fours, and an Ace. Counts 3.

One pair: just that. Counts 1.

Shuffle the pack and deal out five rows of five cards, face up. That's all there is to it. You must now exercise that brain of yours and make a kind of Magic Square of cards. You juggle the cards around to make as many of the Poker hands as you can, horizontally, vertically, or in the two diagonals. Quite sincerely, it is a lot of fun.

I interrupted my writing at that point to deal myself a hand. The final result is on the next page.

You will notice that I have done well, but this is not the only way in which these cards can be arranged: see if you can do better.

Suppose we tot up the score.

Horizontally:

One Heart flush	5
One Club flush	5
One Spade flush	5
One Diamond flush	5

Diagonals:

One straight, 4–5–6–7–8 – and please realize that it could be in any order, e.g. 4–7–5–8–6, as long as the straight is there 12

Vertically:

Three Queens	6
Three Kings	6
Full house, Sixes and Twos . .	10
Full house, Tens and Sevens . .	10
Two pairs, Eights and Fives . .	3
	Total 67

(Incidentally, this has nothing to do with how these combinations would be scored in the game of Poker.)

I felt quite pleased with this result. You can go on like this for hours. Those of you who are crossword fans, here is the card game for you: you will never exhaust the possibilities.

A postscript: if it is your wish to make this Patience game really difficult, then try doing it in what I believe to be the original version; though personally, I have found it less interesting than the one I have described.

The shuffled pack is placed face down before you. One by one you turn up the top twenty-five cards, and having studied each card as it comes along you place it in position in the imaginary five-by-five square.

When all twenty-five cards have been placed, you must end up with as many scoring formations as possible. But no jiggling about; once you have placed a card you leave it where it is, right or wrong.

151

This version calls for great skill and instant planning, because you need to sense the best positions for the cards so as to reach the best result.

Try Poker Patience both ways.

ONE FOUNDATION
Required: 1 pack of 52 cards, a small table

I sat in the sun for most of this July afternoon playing One Foundation. I tried to see if I could finish the game, get it out completely, before my tortoise went back into his little hole in the bank.

My tortoise went back into his little hole, but I hadn't been successful.

This is a Patience game which seems to have been passed by, but I can recommend it highly. It is nice and easy, no complicated rules, but you can become quite clever at it. I may even get it out next time before that tortoise goes home.

Shuffle the pack and deal a row of seven cards face up on the table, or like I did, on a newspaper on the lawn. Deal a second row of seven cards face up from left to right overlapping the first row. Then another, and another, until you have five rows. That's thirty-five cards; place the thirty-sixth card face up below the tableau.

This will be your one foundation card, hence the name; the card you build on. And if you are successful you will build the entire pack on it and have no tableau left. The rest of the pack you place nearby face down in a pile; these are your stock.

Now, the building is done in a very novel way. There are no transfers of cards from one part of the tableau to another, so no descending sequences as in most Patience games. But on the foundation you can build upwards and downwards regardless of suits, as long as the cards are consecutive.

Suppose that the foundation card is a King. You could build downwards on it with Queen, Jack if they are available: or upwards with Ace, Two. If there is no Ten to go on the Jack you could turn back with another Queen and King; if you have built King, Ace, Two and another Two, two Threes, two Fours and a Five were available you could build Two, Three, Two, Three, Four, Five, Four, for example.

But suppose there was no other Five or Three to go on the Four. Then you transfer the top card of the stock to the foundation pile and that gives you a fresh start; away you go again.

The only advice I can give you about strategy is to consider the available cards and look ahead. Sometimes you seem to be making slow progress, sometimes the running is smooth; but I promise you will like this game.

TOWER OF HANOI

Required: nine cards of one suit, Ace to Nine, a small space, lots of determination

Some books on Patience describe this as a fairly easy game, which means that I must be mentally retarded. I find it very difficult, but most intriguing; I hate to give in when I play this one.

Like the puzzle of the same name, played with discs graded in size with holes in the centre which fit on to vertical rods, which you will find described in most books on mathematical recreations, you really have to think about this game; and make lots of moves – if you make mistakes one game could last for ages!

Shuffle the nine cards and lay them out face up in three rows as illustrated (*see* p. 156):

Please study the layout and consider the problem. The idea is to get that lot in a single row, downwards, with the Nine at the top and then Eight, Seven, Six, Five, Four, Three, Two, and the Ace at the bottom.

However, you are allowed to move only the bottom card of any one of the three rows. In our illustration, the Seven, the Nine, or the Eight. And each card can go only under a higher card. So if you move the Seven it can go only under the Nine or Eight. The Eight can go under the Nine. But the Nine cannot go under another card because there isn't a higher one; if, however, you completely clear a row, the Nine can go into the vacant space, so can any other bottom card.

Bearing in mind these simple rules, you begin to move the cards about, trying to manoeuvre the higher cards to the top.

So: set up your cards exactly like the illustration – they were honestly shuffled – as a trial, and let's see how far we can go.

Put the Seven under the Eight, Five under Seven, Three under Five. Move the Nine into the vacant space.

This is a good start (I am playing as I write). Now we are in trouble. The idea is to get the Eight under the Nine, so here we go: Six under Nine, Three under Four, Five under Six, Three under Seven, Four under Five – and you have a clear column. Three under Four, Seven into vacant space, Three under Seven, Four under Eight, Three under Five, Four under Seven, Three under Four, Five under Eight, Three under Six, Four under

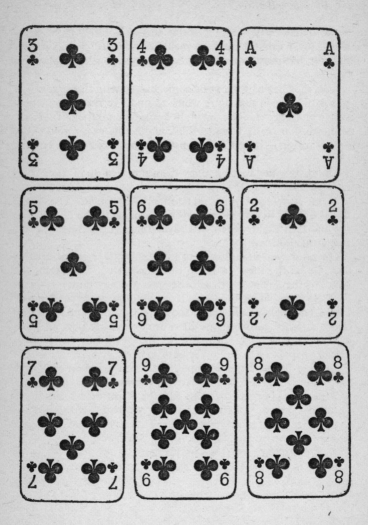

Five, Three under Four, Six under Seven, Three under Six, Four under Nine, Three under Four, Five under Six, Three under Eight, Four under Five, Three under Four, and Eight under Nine.

Well, I have started you on the journey. All you have to do now is to move the Seven, Six, Five, Four, Three, Two, and Ace into place – settle down for a long evening, and the best of British luck.

THE FLOWER GARDEN (*Le Parterre*)

For this excellent Patience game you need one pack of 52 cards. Shuffle well, and deal a little 'fan' of six cards so that they overlap and all the indices are visible. Do this six times, forming a 'flower garden' of six 'beds'; leave some space in the middle of the table for the Aces which will be your foundation cards, i.e. the ones on which you build in suits in ascending order.

The sixteen cards left over are spread out in your hand, or on the table near to you, in a large fan or 'bouquet'.

If there are any Aces in the bouquet, place them in the middle at once. Similarly if there are any Aces exposed at the face of the beds in the garden; but if Aces are buried you have to contrive to get them exposed at the face.

In the garden there are six exposed cards; these can be built on in sequence in descending order, regardless of suit but alternately black and red. You can move complete sequences – but not parts of sequences – from one bed to another to free wanted cards.

From the bouquet you can play any cards you wish, either on to the beds or on to the foundations, but cards once played from the bouquet cannot be taken back again.

Think very carefully before playing cards from the bouquet on to the foundations, in case you may need those cards for building to remove wanted cards from the flower-beds. If you remove a complete bed you can start a new one with a King; this is your only chance of freeing wanted cards which happen to be covered by a King in a bed, because the game is nearly over before a King goes on to a foundation.

If when you first deal out you find Kings and Queens covering the Aces in the beds, you know that your chances of completing the game are slim; for in this Patience game there is no second chance, it's a case of one deal only.

Because there are six beds, and because all the cards are visible, you really have to keep your gardener's eye very watchful for every possible move which will give you a happy result.

I have tried this Patience game on and off for several days now, and have not as yet been successful; perhaps I haven't got green fingers?

DISPLAY
Required: 2 packs of 52 cards, a whacking big table

For this Patience game no great skill is called for, but you have to watch your step because there is so much going on in all directions.

Having shuffled the two packs together, deal the top card over to your left at arm's length, face up. This card, whatever it is, is your corner-stone and the key to the game.

To the right of it you have to build a row of thirteen cards in descending order, regardless of suit or colour. Say your corner-stone is a Three; you continue to the right with Two, Ace, then ('turning the corner') King, Queen, Jack and so on down to Four. You must do this in order: you can't leave a space for the Two and put the Ace down, you must place the Two first.

Below the corner-stone, and below subsequent cards you place in the top row, you build similarly in ascending order: so beneath the Three go Four, Five, Six, and so on.

So, having placed your corner-stone, you turn up cards one at a time from the top of the double pack. If a card can go right into the display, fine; otherwise, cards which cannot be used immediately go into any of three heaps as you wish. You can at any time transfer the exposed card at the face of a heap to the display, so you try to avoid covering a card which you may need very soon with one that you won't need yet awhile.

Don't make the mistake of thinking that it might be a good idea to sort them in the heaps into high, medium, and low cards; that would land you in trouble.

So you carry on building up the big display as far as you can. When you have exhausted the double pack gather up the three heaps of unused cards, turn the pack face down and go through it again – but this time you are allowed only one waste heap, and if you are unsuccessful the game is over. Note, by the way, that you never place more than eight cards in any vertical column, or the display will be impossible. But, if you succeed, you will end up with the whole of the 104 cards arranged in order in eight rows of thirteen cards, a very gratifying display.

Just in case you are at all puzzled, this is what a partly finished game might look like:

```
3 2 A K Q J 10 9 8 7 6 5 4
4 3 2 A K Q J    9 8     5
5   3 2      Q      9     6
6     3       K    10
7     4
```

A relaxing, colourful game; but there is so much you can miss if you are not right on the ball.

PICTURE GALLERY (*also known as* INTRIGUE)
Required: 2 packs of 52 cards

This Patience game is quite fun, and the result if you get it out is most pleasing. You need two packs of cards shuffled together.

To begin with, remove any Queen and place it face up on the table to your left. Holding the stock (the rest of the double pack) face down in your hand you deal cards face up one by one on top of the Queen until one of the following things happens.

If you turn up another Queen, place it to the right of the first one, so beginning a row of Queens: then carry on dealing on top of this Queen. Treat each Queen turned up in the same way until eight Queens complete the row.

If you turn up a Six, place it above the first Queen to begin a row of Sixes.

If you turn up a Five, place it below the first Queen to begin a row of Fives.

So you watch out for three denominations, Queens, Sixes, and Fives.

Now: as you deal you can build upwards on the Sixes, Seven, Eight, Nine and so on, until a Jack tops the pile, then stop. Build upwards regardless of suit or colour. Similarly, you build downwards on the Fives, Four, Three and so on; when you arrive at the Ace you top it with a King. This is known as 'going around the corner'.

You can at any time take the exposed card from the face of a pile on top of a Queen and add it to an upper or lower pile in order to build; naturally you do this whenever possible.

So you are dealing away merrily, watching madly for every chance to build, trying to clear away the cards covering the Queens; and as the number of Queens increases you have more and more points to watch. With luck you end up with a picture gallery of Jacks, Queens, and Kings.

A simple plot, a layout which grows excitingly, plenty to keep your eyes and hands busy, and if you are successful, a delightful result in technicolor. This is one of my favourites.

CLOCK PATIENCE
Required: 1 pack of 52 cards, plenty of table room

This game doesn't need any brains at all, it's just a 12-to-1 gamble.

Shuffle the pack, and deal the cards face down in a circle like the numerals on a clock face, with a thirteenth card in the middle. Keep on dealing round in this way until all the pack is dealt and you have four cards in each heap.

The game is very simple. Turn face up the top card of the middle heap. If this should be a King, put it face up underneath the middle heap; if it is a Six, put it face up under the heap at six o'clock; if it is a Queen, which of course counts as 12, put it face up under the twelve o'clock heap, and so on. Jack counts as 11.

Turn up the top card of whichever heap you have placed the face-up card under. Say it is a Three; put it under the three o'clock heap and turn the top card of that face up; if this is a Nine put it under the nine o'clock heap and turn the top card of that face up; if that is a King it goes under the middle heap. And you carry on in this way as long as you can.

To win, you must have all the 'numerals' round the clock dial in their correct places before the last of the four Kings turns up. As the man said, it is 12 to 1. The moment you have four Kings face up in the middle you are through – gather up the cards, shuffle well, and start all over again.

Time, gentlemen, please!

GRANDFATHER'S CLOCK
Required: 2 packs of 52 cards, plenty of table space

I have given this Patience game this name to distinguish it from the simpler Clock Patience which you will find on p 162. This is one of the most difficult and complicated of all Patience games, but you will derive great satisfaction from getting it out; incidentally, it is well over a hundred years old.

Before you shuffle the two packs together, pick out the cards shown in the 'clock-face' on the left of the illustrated layout (164). The clock on the left shows how the game begins, and that on the right shows how it ends if you are successful. The cards visible on the right are of course the top or face cards of each completed pile.

So you make the clock-face on the left, beginning with the Six of Clubs at one o'clock, the Seven of Hearts at two o'clock, and so on, as illustrated. Note that the King is omitted.

Shuffle the remaining cards well, and beginning at one o'clock (the Six of Clubs) place a fan of three cards beside it, and so on all the way round to the Five of Diamonds at twelve o'clock, making an 'outer circle' of fans. In the illustration I have shown only one fan of three cards, below the Jack of Hearts at six o'clock.

Having completed the layout with the twelve fans round the clock-face, you are ready to begin. You can use the face, or exposed card of a fan to build on the twelve foundations – the clock-face cards – in the same suits, in ascending values, only until you reach the true time on the clock-face, and note that in many cases you build 'around the corner': for example, on the Jack of Hearts you build the Queen of Hearts, then the King, the Ace, the Two, and so on until the foundation is completed with the Six of Hearts.

The twelve o'clock pile, by the way, ends with the King of Diamonds, not the Queen.

Play as many cards as you can from fans on to the clock-face. To release hidden cards you can transfer single cards or sequences from one fan to another, in suits and in descending order. When you reach stalemate, that is, when there are no more moves you can make, begin to turn up cards from the stock, the remaining cards in your hand. Wherever there are less than three cards in a fan, make it up to three with the next cards

PLAYER'S VIEW FROM HERE

from the stock, beginning at one o'clock and working round clockwise.

Any time the fans are made up and there are no further moves to be made, deal cards one at a time from the stock on to a waste heap in the centre of the clock-face. The face card of this heap may at any time be played on to a foundation where it fits, but not on to the fans; when, however, transfers bring a fan to less than three cards, you make it up to three from the stock.

So if your game is successful you end up with all the cards absorbed into the clock-face. You are not allowed to turn the waste heap over and have a second run through; you go through the stock once only, and that is that. To bring the game to a successful conclusion depends partly on luck, of course, but also very largely on the way you manage your fans. Like a fan-dancer.

SPACES AND ACES
Required: 1 pack of 52 cards, plenty of table space

I tried this Patience game under its original name of 'Spaces' and found it impossible to handle, but by making a slight alteration I think that we now have something to tax the brainy ones.

Shuffle the pack and deal it into four rows of thirteen cards, face up.

With the whole pack staring you in the face, remove the Aces, wherever they may be. This of course leaves four empty spaces. Now place an Ace at the left-hand end of each row. You have some scope for judgement here: if for example there is a predominance of Diamonds in one row, it will probably help to place the Ace of Diamonds at the left of this row. It may be that one row ends with a King at the right-hand end: this is where you will eventually want it, so it would be a good idea to put the appropriate Ace at the other end, especially if the row contains other cards of the same suit.

The idea is to finish up with four rows each consisting of one complete suit in the correct order, the Ace at the left and the King at the right. Four neat rows of Diamonds, Clubs, Hearts, and Spades, though not necessarily in that order.

Having placed your Aces, study the lay-out. There are now fourteen cards or spaces in each row and the number must never exceed fourteen. You have four spaces; if it happened that, when you first dealt out the cards two Aces came out side by side, then you may have adjoining spaces, a double space.

You can move the cards around to achieve your object of four completed rows; any card from anywhere can be moved into an empty space, provided – and this is essential – there is a lower-value card of the same suit on the left of the space.

Suppose, for example, that to the left of one space you have a Three of Diamonds. Any higher Diamond than the Three can be moved into this space. You look around and notice that the Eight of Diamonds lies to the right of the Ace of Spades. Move the Eight into the space next to the Three. The card you want in the space you have just created is of course the Two of Spades, so find it and place it there and you have made a start with the Spades row.

Perhaps the card now to the right of the Two of Spades can

be moved into a space; if so the Three of Spades can now go into position.

But don't move cards aimlessly, it will get you nowhere. Plan every move, just as you would a move in Chess. Look ahead.

Be particularly wary of the Kings. They can get you into difficulties. Obviously, a space to the right of a King is useless to you because there is no card of greater value with which you can fill it. So you will have to get the King out of the way, preferably to the end of his proper row. Then you will have a double space; think in terms of both the cards with which you will fill it.

As you play, points of strategy will occur to you, and you will be able to plan your play several moves ahead.

The fun really begins when you have the suits beginning to look in some kind of order and you have to juggle the last few cards into position. When all seems hopeless you may suddenly spot a series of moves which will get one card into position, and the rest will follow. Success! But if you arrive at a situation where you can get no further, pack it all up, shuffle the cards thoroughly, and start again.

In this slightly altered form I can promise you hours of fun with this particular game.

THE SULTAN

Required: 2 packs of cards, fair amount of table space

Here is a very old Patience game, and for my money the best thing about it is the lay-out.

Remove the eight Kings from the packs and arrange them as shown in the illustration below. Notice how the Ace of Hearts is placed between the two Kings of Clubs.

Shuffle the two packs together, and on either side of the Kings deal out a column of cards as shown. These two columns are known as the 'divan'.

The idea is to build in ascending order, in suits, ending up with all the Queens, on all the Kings except the King of Hearts – hence the Ace of Hearts.

So as soon as you have an Ace you place it on the appropriate King, and follow with the Two and so on. Whenever a card from the divan can be played, it is used and its space filled with the next card from the stock.

The double pack, or stock, is turned up one card at a time on to the table forming a waste heap, suitable cards being built on to the foundations as they turn up. When the stock is used up the waste heap is shuffled and dealt through again – and if this does not get you out, you can shuffle it and deal through it yet again.

If you are successful, the sultan – the King of Hearts – will end up with his 'harem' around him.

This is not the most exciting of Patience games, but I have included it just for its novelty.

THE BATTLE OF THE LADIES
Required: 1 pack of 52 cards

This little Patience game is attractive for its plot, and for the lay-out which is simple.

From a pack of 52 cards take out the four Queens and place them in a row face up. Also take out the Jacks; place the Jack of Hearts directly above the four Queens and discard the other three Jacks.

Shuffle the rest of the pack, and then deal three face-up cards on each side of the Jack of Hearts in a triangular formation. Of course, you could have two rows of three if you wish, but I think that an attractive lay-out or tableau always adds to the visual enjoyment of any Patience game.

You now have to build on the foundation cards, the four Queens, in the same suits in ascending order: so you start 'round the corner' with the King, then Ace, Two, Three, and so on until you arrive at the Ten. The first Queen to reach Ten wins the Jack of Hearts.

You can also build on the six exposed cards – those in the triangles on either side of the Jack of Hearts – in descending order in alternate colours. You can transfer one of these cards on to another as long as you follow this rule; and you can transfer a sequence of cards. And the exposed cards in these six positions can go on to the foundations when the time comes. Whenever there is an empty space you can fill it with the top card of the stock, the face-down pack in your hand.

When no further movement is possible, deal another six cards from the stock on to the six positions, so covering up whatever building you have been able to do. Again, make any moves you can. And so on.

There is one strict rule which must be observed. You must be impartial, you must allow any Queen to gain any advantage she can. If, for example, there are cards which can be built on a Queen she must have them, even if the manipulation of those cards stops another Queen from getting a card which she needs. In other words, when you build on a Queen you must at that point do as much as possible for that Queen to the exclusion of the others.

When all cards have been dealt and the Queens are still battling, you are allowed to pick up the six heaps in order as dealt, turn the pack over and deal six cards out as at the beginning. This you may do twice, i.e. three deals altogether. If you are still unlucky you, along with the Queens, have lost.

And may the best Queen win.

PUSS IN THE CORNER
Required: 1 pack of 52 cards

A simple Patience game, easy to get out if you use your noddle.

Remove the four Aces from the pack and place them together face up in a square in the middle of the table.

The idea is to build upwards on these Aces, not in suits but in colour. So a Four of Clubs may be put on to either a Three of Clubs or a Three of Spades. The red cards are treated in the same way. But having got this game out after a few tries, make it a little more difficult by building on the Aces in suits only.

Now for the game. Having placed the Aces, hold the balance of the pack face down in your hand and turn up the cards one at a time. Cards which do not go straight into the building – for example, a Two would go straight on to an Ace – are placed face up at one or other of the four corners of the square formed by the Aces, forming four waste piles from which you can at any time play the face card on to a foundation when it fits.

The placing of the unsuitable cards is the secret of this game. Try to keep cards of about the same values in the same heap: at the start, for example, you would put the Threes and Fours in one pile, the Fives, Sixes, and Sevens in another, the Eights, Nines, and Tens in another, and the court cards in the fourth. After you have transferred the Threes and Fours to the foundations you will have a spare space which you could use to keep cards you will shortly be needing, or to avoid covering a card you will need soon. You must think ahead.

When you have gone once through the pack, building on to the Ace foundation piles whenever possible, pick up the waste piles in the most advantageous order, assemble them into a pack, turn it face down and deal through it again. If you have assembled the pack so that the pile of lowest cards is now at the top and the highest at the bottom, you will find that with a bit of luck the cards go nicely into place and your game will come out. But note that this time you deal into only one face-up waste pile, not four corner piles, and you can only redeal once.

A good game, this, and you have to be a bit astute: it is not all a matter of luck.

PAIRS
Required: 1 pack of 52 cards, little table space

This is a simple Patience game which I managed to get out at the fifth attempt the first time I played it. I am sure that you can do better.

All you need is a pack of 52 cards, and very little table space – in fact, the beauty of this game and its variations which I shall describe below is that you can play them on a large book or something of the kind, on your lap.

Deal three rows, each of three cards, face up. Whenever you see two cards of the same value, pick them up and put them aside, filling their places with another two cards from the pack in your hand.

The idea is to use up the entire pack at one go. This game can run smoothly, or it can come to an abrupt stop with all the nine cards of different values and no pairs to pick out. Then you have to shuffle the cards and start again.

I tried four rows of three cards, and it came out without difficulty, so I understand why it is that only three rows are allowed.

There are two variations of this game which you may like to try for a change. The first is Elevens. It is played exactly the same as Pairs, except that instead of picking up pairs of matching cards, you pick out two cards whose pips add up to eleven: Ace and Ten, Seven and Four, and so on. Picture cards count as spaces, that is to say that whenever a court card turns up you cover it with the next card from the pack; then when you take out a card as part of an 'eleven' you also take any court cards that lie beneath it.

Elevens is a bit easier to get out than Pairs; better, I think, and more interesting, is the other variation, Thirteens. Here the picture cards enter into it: the value of a Jack is 11, a Queen 12, a King 13. You pick out pairs of cards adding up to thirteen, Nine and Four, Six and Seven, Queen and Ace, and so on: A King is thirteen so it comes out on its own.

173

MAGIC PATIENCE
Required: 1 pack of 52 cards, table space

I showed the Calculation game (*see* p 139) to a friend of mine and it reminded him of this very intriguing and really magical kind of Patience.

No element of chance or judgement enters into it, but you have to be absolutely accurate in the play or else there is no magical climax and you have failed.

Lay out on the table an Ace, a Two, a Three, and a Four of any suits – suits and colours are immaterial throughout.

Now, holding the remainder of your shuffled pack of 52 cards face down in your hand, you turn up cards singly from the top of the pack into a face-up pile.

Look out for cards which are double the value of your four foundation cards – that is, of course, Two, Four, Six, and Eight – and as they turn up lay them below the appropriate cards, a Two below the Ace, and so on.

Having done this, carry on turning up cards one at a time, this time looking out for cards whose value is the total of each pair of upper and lower cards: a Three for the Ace and Two, a Six for the Two and Four, a Nine for the Three and Six, and a Queen – Jack, Queen, and King count as Eleven, Twelve, and Thirteen respectively – for the Four and Eight. As they turn up lay them in the appropriate places on top of the lower cards.

When you come to the end of the pack pick up your face-up pile, turn it face down and start dealing through it again.

Having completed that row, continue in the same way with the next row with cards equalling the total value of the upper and lower cards: except that when the total exceeds thirteen, for example Queen (12) and Four totals sixteen, you deduct thirteen from the total. So on the Queen, the fourth card in that last row, you would place a Three (16 − 13 = 3).

Carry on like this, turning over the waste pile whenever necessary, and when you have used up all the pack you will have, provided that you have played correctly, four piles each topped with a King below your original foundation of Ace, Two, Three, and Four.

So far, so good. Now place each of the four piles upon the card above it, the first on the Ace, second on the Two and so on. Gather up the four resulting piles in this way: put the fourth on the third, these two on the second, the three on the first. Square up the cards without disturbing their order and turn the pack face downwards.

Now deal out the first thirteen cards from the top of the face-down pack from left to right into a row of thirteen cards.

Deal the next thirteen on top of them in this way: the first on to the second card, the next on the fourth, and so on, dealing on to alternate cards; when you come to the twelfth you skip the thirteenth of course and come back to the first, then third, fifth, and so on. So you will go twice along the row, ending on the last card.

Next lot: similarly except that you cover every third card, skipping two. Start on number 3, then 6, 9, 12, back to the start, skipping two, so a card on number 2 and so on. This time you will have to go along the row three times and, as before, end on the last card in the row.

You have thirteen cards left. These go on each fourth card, skipping three: on number 4, number 8, number 12, skip three and back to number 3, and so on. The last card of the pack will complete the thirteenth pile.

Now assemble the thirteen packets carefully, making sure not to disturb the order of the cards, in this way: the first on the second, these two on the third, and so on. You finish up with the entire pack face down on the table in one pile.

Now comes the vitally important things you have to do, so be sure to do it correctly. You pronounce the magic word 'Abracadabra' out loud – better practise a bit, to make sure you have it right – at the same time waving your left hand over the pack in the form of a figure eight.

Having done this, pick up the face-down pack. Spell the values of the cards out loud, in order, dealing a card on to the table face down for each letter, but turning face up the card which falls on the last letter. So you spell 'A' (card face down), 'C' (card face down), 'E' (card face up). Carry on like this: 'T – W – O', 'T – H – R – E – E', and so on up to Jack, Queen, King.

And if you have played the whole game accurately the result will surprise you, and anyone who happens to be watching you.

If it doesn't – well, you made a mistake somewhere. Or, of course, you failed to pronounce that magic spell correctly.

Come to think of it, perhaps this ought to be called the Magic Spell.

Games of Patience, once you have played a few, become a bit of a drug. By trying out so many on your behalf I have become completely 'hooked.'

I read the other day in the *Daily Express* that a Mr Lewis Sutter, of New York, has played 150,000 games of Solitaire – that's what the Americans call Patience – since he retired ten years ago. He has kept a record of every game, and has filled ten bulky ledgers. That's being hooked, if you like.

A friend of mine who lives in Mill Hill, Mrs Jane Bratt, has shown me her favourite Patience games. I am sure that they have names, but she does not remember them; so I have taken the extreme liberty of inventing titles for them.

SUPER FLOWER GARDEN
Required: 1 pack of 52 cards

Deal seventeen fans of three cards each as artistically as you can: you will need plenty of space. You will have one card left over; just place it face up on the table.

For the moment you have to consider only the exposed cards of the seventeen fans, and that one left-over card.

Any Aces which are exposed must be put in front of you in a row as your foundation cards, to be built on in suits upwards.

Kings may not be moved. No spaces must be filled. You may build downwards on exposed cards regardless of suit, but only one card may be moved at a time.

There is so much to look at, and so many possibilities to consider, that you are kept very busy indeed.

Never cover up a card until you are sure that you could not have made a better move. When all possible moves have been made, and your foundations are still incomplete, you may gather up the cards which are not on the foundations, shuffle, and deal in threes again. If this second deal does not get you out you may deal once more; and if you are not successful this time you really have lost – no more deals.

The nearest game to this is *La Belle Lucie*, in which the rules are not so strict. Super Flower Garden is a super game; you really have to be on your toes.

(I am describing Mrs Bratt's games rather briefly, because I assume that by now the general principles of Patience are familiar to you.)

FOUR ROWS OF FOURS
Required: 2 packs of 52 cards

Two packs of cards are shuffled together. Deal four cards, over-lapping, in a row; leave a space, and then four more cards in a row, overlapping – all face up.

Do this four times: that's eight lots of four. The seventy-two cards left over make up the stock or *talon*.

You have eight free or exposed cards to consider. You must work to liberate the Aces, all eight of them, which when they are free are put in two columns between the fours.

The Aces are the foundations and are built on upwards in suits. Exposed cards can be built on in sequence, in descending order, regardless of suits. After all possible moves have been made, and any available Aces freed and transferred to the middle, any spaces created may be filled with Kings.

One by one cards are dealt from the stock on to a waste heap. These cards can be built on to the foundations, the Aces, or on to the fours if this manoeuvre helps to release wanted cards. Sequences can be moved from one four to another. The stock can be gone through once only.

Excellent game, this.

THREE ROWS OF EIGHT
Required: 2 packs of 52 cards (thoroughly shuffled)

Deal three rows of eight cards each, face up, not overlapping in any way. Any Aces must be taken out and discarded; they have no further purpose.

Now the spaces left vacant must be filled in a special way. In the first row spaces may be filled with Twos only; in the second row, with Threes only; in the third row, with Fours only.

The stock, the remainder of the double pack, is dealt one card at a time on to a waste heap in the usual way.

If there are no Twos, Threes, or Fours available at the start, you have to wait until you can fill the spaces from the stock. As soon as you have a Two in the first row you can begin to build on it, regardless of suits, but you do so in steps of three: that is, on the Two go a Five, then an Eight, then a Jack.

Similarly, in the second row you build on the Threes with a Six, Nine, and Queen; and in the fourth row, build on the Fours with a Seven, Ten, and finally a King.

To help you, by keeping useful cards handy, you may build in descending order regardless of suits on any cards not already involved in the building-up. You may make spaces by transferring non-involved cards for building in descending order in the same way. But be careful how you do this, because you can block yourself badly.

The stock is dealt through once only. With luck, you end up with all the Jacks, Queens, and Kings in spectacular array. A very good game.

UNLUCKY THIRTEEN
Required: 2 packs of 52 cards

This is the last of Mrs Jane Bratt's Patience games.

Thoroughly shuffle two packs together. Deal thirteen cards in a row, face up. Under this row deal a row of eight cards; then another eight, overlapping the first eight; then yet another eight, overlapping again. So what you have is actually a row of thirteen cards with eight columns of three below.

Now deal the next card, face up, above the row of thirteen. This, whatever it may be, is your first foundation card. Suppose it is a Seven; then all the other Sevens become foundation cards, to be built on in suits in ascending order, going 'round the corner' when you come to the Kings so that each foundation will end up with a Six on top. Or, of course, whatever it may be according to the denomination of the first card.

The rest of the pack becomes the *talon* or stock. From this you turn up cards one at a time, forming not more than eight waste heaps, into which you distribute as carefully as possible cards which can be used later. You need not in fact make all the eight waste heaps immediately, but only as convenient.

Now consider the scene. Any exposed Sevens (or whatever your first foundation card was) must be put above as foundations. Any exposed cards, whether they are the face or exposed cards of the eight columns, or cards from the 'unlucky thirteen', or the exposed top cards of the waste heaps, or, of course, the next card from the stock, can be built on to the foundations at any time.

Any trapped Sevens must be freed as soon as possible. This is done – and, of course, the same applies to cards needed later for building on the foundations – by transferring cards from one column to another, singly or in complete sequences, using exposed cards from the top of the waste heaps or the next card from the stock to help out: but always building on the columns in descending order, irrespective of suits.

This does not apply to the unlucky thirteen; no building on these cards is allowed. They can be used only for building on the foundations, and when one is removed the space must be filled with the next card from the stock.

Spaces in the eight columns may be filled from stock, from the exposed top cards of the waste heaps, or by transfer of a single card or a complete sequence from another column.

There is plenty to watch, and plenty to do all the time. When you feel that you have made all possible moves, and filled all the spaces, you deal one by one more cards from stock on to your waste heaps. When you have gone through the stock once and have not been successful in completing your foundations, you may collect the waste heaps and deal once more; but that is the end.

A very pleasant game, this, and it comes out fairly easily – if you keep your eyes open.

Simple card tricks

SIMPLE CARD TRICKS

As this book is about card games, and as I am by profession a magician, I must take this opportunity of telling you the secrets of a few simple card tricks with which you can amuse and mystify your friends. So, let me begin with:

CLAIRVOYANCE

Secretly remove from a pack of cards a complete sequence of one suit, Ace to Ten, and put these cards on top of the pack, Ace at the top and so on downwards to the Ten.

Inform your audience that you intend to demonstrate your powers of clairvoyance.

You proceed to deal off the top ten cards in a row, face downwards. Your audience knows nothing of the pre-arrangement, of course.

In the illustration I have shown the cards face upwards, so that you can follow the mechanics of the trick.

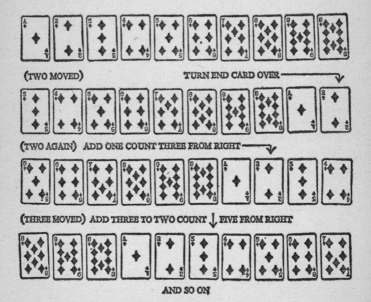

(TWO MOVED)   TURN END CARD OVER ————————↴

(TWO AGAIN) ADD ONE COUNT THREE FROM RIGHT ————↴

(THREE MOVED) ADD THREE TO TWO COUNT ↓ FIVE FROM RIGHT

AND SO ON

184

Ask someone to move one or more cards from the left of the row to the right, one at a time, while your back is turned. He can if he wishes, having moved the cards, adjust the row so that you cannot judge the number by comparing the position of the cards with a mark on the table, or some other means.

When he has finished, you turn round. With a great show of concentrating, you announce that not only do you know how many cards have been moved, but you will turn up a card which will indicate the number. So saying, you turn over the card at the extreme right of the row, which turns out to be a Two – and this is the number of cards which have been moved.

You will easily understand this first revelation, I am sure, by studying the illustration.

You turn your back again, and more cards are secretly moved: let's say, for example, two again. When you turn round, remember the previous number, two; add one to it, making three; count to the third card from the right, and lo and behold! the Two turns up again.

Turn your back again, this time carrying the previous numbers, three and two, in your mind, which add up to five. When you turn round again, deliberate for a moment and simply count to the fifth card from the right; turn it up, and suppose that it's a three, then you know that three cards have been moved.

For your next bit of clairvoyance you remember the five and the three, making a total of eight; so you already know that the number of cards moved this time will be revealed by the eighth card from the right.

Bow to the applause, and stop while you are still good.

THE MYSTERIOUS COUNT

Once again ten consecutive cards, from Ace to Ten, are removed from a pack of cards and secretly arranged in the order shown in this illustration:

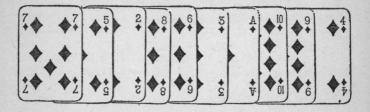

When the cards have been arranged correctly, pick them up and turn them face downwards and you are ready to perform.

Hold the little package in your left hand as if you were about to deal. Spell out aloud 'A', sliding one card off the top of the packet and placing it at the bottom. Then 'C', placing the next card underneath; then 'E', placing another card underneath. Then say 'Ace' and turn the next card face up on the table. Sure enough, it will be the Ace. Now spell out 'T, W, O' in the same way, turning the next card face up; it will be the Two, and so on, until you have only one card left, the Ten.

Practice this a couple of times, and then you are ready at the right moment to mystify your friends.

It occurs to me that it would be a good idea to do this little trick before, or after, the previous trick, 'Clairvoyance', on page 184, because you use the same cards, Ace to Ten, for both.

HOW MANY PIPS?

This first-rate trick is performed while you, the performer, are out of the room; or it can even be done over the telephone, which makes it very mystifying indeed, and will convince your friends that you are a mind-reader.

You need a full pack of 52 cards, the Joker being removed. The pack is shuffled by a member of your audience, who is asked to place the top card face up on the table. This he does. You point out that the card turned up is (for example) a Seven, so he is to deal five cards face downwards on to the Seven; thus making a total of twelve. Seven pips on the card plus the five cards dealt on to it, understand?

You go on to explain that you will leave the room while the dealer uses up all the cards in this manner, making twelve every time. A picture card is to be treated as a Ten, so only two cards would be dealt on to it to make twelve. If at the end there are not enough cards left to complete the operation, then the balance which won't make a twelve are to be put on one side.

So while you are out of the room, the following happens. The pack is shuffled, and the first card dealt on to the table face up is, we'll suppose, the Queen of Diamonds. On to the Queen are dealt two cards face down. Next card face up is, say, the Ten of Spades; on to this go another two cards. Next face-up card is, say, the Ace of Hearts; so eleven cards are dealt on to it. Next the Five of Diamonds; on to this go seven cards. Now the Three of Hearts; nine cards go on this. Next, the Six of Spades; add six cards. Next the King of Clubs: add two cards. The next card turned face up is, we'll suppose, the Three of Spades, but as there are only five cards left in the pack there aren't enough to make the number up to twelve. So the dealing out is finished, and in this case there are six cards left over, which are put aside. (There won't always be six, of course; there could be none at all, or any number up to eleven.)

The performer, that's you, is now told that all is ready for him. Without coming into the room you ask the following questions. How many heaps on the table? In our example the answer is seven. You always mentally subtract four from the number of heaps, so in this case the remainder is three. Now you multiply this remainder by thirteen – it's not difficult to do this in your head, because the remainder is always a small number.

So now we have $3 \times 13 = 39$. Now you ask: how many cards are left over? In this case the answer is six. Add the six to the thirty-nine, and you get 45.

Now you say: 'Please, counting all court cards as ten, add up the total number of pips on the face-up cards. You will find the total to be – 45!' And sure enough, it is.

As I said at the beginning, this is a first-rate trick: just try it over the telephone.

THE INNER CIRCLE

Here is a puzzling little item which will keep 'them' worried for a long time.

Arrange nine cards in a circle, face down. The puzzle is this: you tap cards with your finger, going clockwise round the circle, counting 'One, Two, Three' – and turn the third card face up. Now you start again on another card, 'One, Two, Three' and again turn the third card face up. You continue to do this, always tapping consecutive cards, and always beginning on a face-down card and ending on a face-down card which you turn up; right through to the end, until there is only one face-down card left, which you just turn up. Or if you prefer you can tap as before, except that of course this last time you have to start on a face-up card.

Try this before I let you in to the secret. You can't do it, can you?

The secret is simple, ingenious. Having started as in the illustration on page 190, you have tapped One, Two, and Three, and turned up Three. Now, remember where you started ('One') and count two cards back for your next starter – position Four on the illustration. Count One, Two, Three and turn up the original number One. Remember position Four and again count two cards back, which will be position Five in the illustration; tap One, Two, Three and turn up the card marked Four. And so on.

Keep this up, and success will be yours – and your reputation as a wonder-man getting greater and greater.

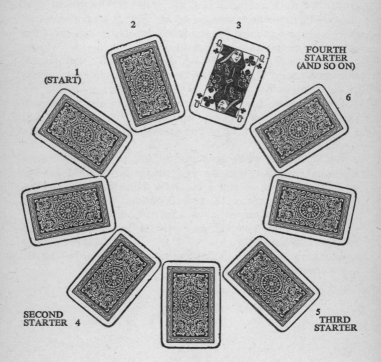

FIND THE PAIR

This is my favourite self-working trick for parties, and it is as old as the hills.

The secret is based on four Latin words: MUTUS NOMEN COCIS DEDIT. The effect is this. Announce that you are about to do a bit of divination. Deal ten pairs of cards on to the table. The pack was shuffled first, of course, and the pairs are placed so that each card of each pair can be easily seen.

You ask a member of the audience just to think of any one pair of cards without giving you any hint as to which he has chosen; he has ten pairs to choose from.

When a pair has been selected, by thought only, you pick up the pairs of cards in any order but without separating the pairs.

You begin to place the cards one by one, face up, in various positions on the table, ending up with four rows of five cards each; telling your audience that you are working on a magic square.

Now you ask the person who is thinking of the cards to point to the row or rows (horizontally) that his cards are in. Whichever he points to, you immediately tell him the names of the two cards he thought of. Very effective, this.

Now try this out without an audience. Put a sheet of wrapping paper on the table and with a pencil or pen mark out four rows with those Latin words like this, spacing them out so that each letter occupies the space of a card:

M U T U S
N O M E N
C O C I S
D E D I T

That is how you must remember the words, which mean 'Mutus' (whoever he was) 'gave a name to the Coci' (whoever they were). Here you have the aid, but of course when performing you won't have the paper to help you, you have to visualize the positions of the letters, exactly as I have shown.

Now deal out ten pairs of cards, remember one pair, then collect the pairs in any order without separating any of them.

Now: place the first card on the letter M, then the next card on the other M. That's one pair seen to. Put the next card on the letter U, and the next on the other U – and so on with all the other letters.

You will notice that there are ten pairs of letters. And remembering the Latin sentence, it is easy to remember where they are. So that if you are told that the pair of cards being thought of are both in the top row, they must be those covering your imaginary letters U. If they are in the first two rows, they must be the cards covering the M's. If in the first and last rows, they must be the cards covering the letters T. Is that clear?

The moment you have memorized the words *Mutus Nomen Cocis Dedit* you can do the trick: and if you have read this article you must have learnt them by now.

Now try the trick with imaginary letters on the table. You will find it delightfully simple, and a great reputation-maker.

'Find the pair' need not be performed for one person only. You can have any number of people thinking of pairs of cards, all at the same time, and one by one you tell them what cards they are thinking of. It's just as easy, and ten times more effective.

Postscript: After I had written the foregoing, it occurred to me that you might prefer to use some alternative mnemonic to the ancient traditional MUTUS NOMEN COCIS DEDIT.

Not many young people seem to learn Latin at school these days, as I did; in any case, you may find something a bit more modern easier to memorize.

There is another old one: DAVID LOVEL IN YON ABBEY.

But after playing about with the idea for an hour or so I came up with the following:

> APPLE LOOKS TASTY, KENNY
> A FAKE; FLYNN LOOKS TESTY
> HELLO TESSA, HAPPY TOMMY
> FADED SHOES, HAPPY FOLLY.

And one that I think is better than these, ADAMS PIPES MERRY DITTY.

But perhaps you can do better still? Have a go: if you are successful you can pride yourself on having something exclusive!

192

PREDICTION

As a member of the Magic Circle I come across many oddities in the way of card tricks and games. This little item, which I have called Prediction, was shown to me some time ago; I never found out just who invented or discovered it. Perhaps no one did: perhaps it just happened.

Shuffle a pack well. Think of any combination of two cards, for example a Ten and a Three. Now begin to deal cards from the top of the pack face up.

And if you have predicted correctly, sure enough, a Ten and a Three will fall consecutively!

You will be amazed to discover how often you will be successful. It might of course happen more than once in the course of a complete deal, though this is unlikely.

If you are a bit of a mathematician, you can perhaps work out why it is likely to happen and what chances you have of bringing off our prediction. You see, there are four Tens, and any one of the four Threes can fall on either side of them, giving eight chances. I have worked it out that the odds are 32 to 19 in favour of success – but I could be wrong. See what you make it.

If you would like to bewilder a friend and not tell him how, try this. Ask him to name any two values, say a King and a Two. Let him shuffle the pack and hand it to you. You deal the cards one by one face up and with a bit of luck, up come a King and a Two together. Perhaps he will bet you a drink that it won't happen. Take the bet, for the odds are well in your favour.

And if you are unlucky the first time, give the pack another shuffle and try again.

A Selected Bibliography

The Pan Book of Card Games. Hubert Phillips. (Pan Books Ltd, London.)

The Penguin Hoyle. Hubert Phillips. (Penguin Books Ltd, Harmondsworth.)

The Complete Patience Book. Basil Dalton. (Pan Books Ltd, London.)

The Pocket Book of Games. Albert H. Morehead. (Pocket Books Inc, New York.)

Card Games for One. George F. Hervey. (Teach Yourself Books. English Universities Press Ltd, London.)

Card Games for Two. Kenneth Konstam. (Teach Yourself Books. As above.)

Enquire Within. Compiled by Kenneth Konstam. (Thomas de la Rue & Co. Ltd, London.)

First Book of Bridge. Alfred Sheinwold. (Faber and Faber Ltd, London.)

Contract Bridge Made Easy. Josephine Culbertson. (As above.)

26 Round Card Games. Clifford Montrose. (Universal Publications Ltd, London.)

Popular Card Games. B. H. Wood and F. R. Ings. (W. Foulsham & Co. Ltd, London.)

31 Patience Games. Tom King. (As above.)

Games. B. C. Westall. (Associated Newspapers Ltd, London.)

Most of the above are inexpensive paperbacks. I can't tell you which are currently obtainable; you will have to ask around. And you should be warned: no two books describe any one game in quite the same way. That's part of the charm of card games: all the variations.

And don't breathe a word to a soul, but you may find lots of sheer errors. I hope you won't find any in this book.

To conclude, a few books which are nice collectors' pieces. You are unlikely to find these on sale – but who knows, you might.

Hoyle's Card Games Modernised. Professor Hoffmann. 1909.

The Illustrated Book of Patience Games. Professor Hoffmann. (Translated from the German.) (George Routledge & Sons Ltd. 1901.)

Play your cards right!

Bridge for Beginners 40p
Victor Mollo and Nico Gardener

This excellent book is for the complete beginner. It explains every phase of bridge step by step – the rules, scoring, the conventions and techniques of bidding and card play. And there are exercises after each lesson to help the reader develop his newly-acquired skill.

The Complete Patience Book 40p
Basil Dalton

Here are three best-selling Patience books for the price of one! Incorporating the author's *Games of Patience*, *Double Pack Patience* and *Patience Problems and Puzzles*, it includes over one hundred different games of Patience. Some are easy, some are difficult – all provide a unique form of mental exercise and entertainment.

You can buy these and other Pan books from booksellers and newsagents; or direct from the following address:

Pan Books Cavaye Place London SW10 9PG
Please send purchase price plus 10p postage

While every effort is made to keep prices low, it is sometimes necessary to increase prices at short notice. Pan Books reserve the right to show on covers new retail prices which may differ from those advertised in the text or elsewhere